101 ACTIVITIES to ignite Collaboration, BOOST CREATIVITY, and fuel innovation

Written by Karen Tilstra, PhD
Art by Patrick O'Connor

BRIGHTRAY
PUBLISHING®

We help busy professionals write and publish their stories
to distinguish themselves and their brands.

(407) 287-5700 | Winter Park, FL
info@BrightRay.com | www.BrightRay.com

ISBN: 978-1-956464-42-9

Published in the United States of America.
BrightRay Publishing ® 2023

Table of Contents

Why This Book?

Section One
Sparking Community

Section Two
Igniting a Culture That Emboldens Creativity

Section Three
Applied Improv

Section Four
Energizing Stokes

Section Five
Tools For Leading Change

Section Eight
Reflection Tools

Bonus Section Nine
Knock-Their-Socks-Off Presentations

*This book is dedicated to
Richard Regan Paul—a true
creative from the ground up!*

Why this Book?

Welcome to *101*! We're thrilled you're here if you're looking for ways to rev up your team's creativity, collaboration, and energy. This book is jam-packed with tried-and-true ideas that will do just that and more!

We want to clear up one thing from the get-go: we don't call the activities in this book "icebreakers." Nope, we prefer to call them "cognitive engagements." Just like icebreakers, these engagements get people talking and connected, but they go even further. They help raise awareness, deepen learning, and create shared experiences among groups. And the best part? They can quickly shift the way individuals and groups operate, expanding everyone's point of view and understanding. In short, these cognitive engagements have the potential to transform old, *ego*-centric systems into new, dynamic, *eco*-centric systems built on collaboration and co-creation.

We firmly believe that everyone has untapped creative and leadership potential, but sometimes, it just needs to be unlocked. That's where this book comes in. We've curated a collection of cognitive engagements to ignite your team's creativity and unlock its full potential. It's time to unleash your team's talents and take things to the next level! So, are you ready to access this untapped talent? Let's dive in and find out!

Rationale for These 101 Cognitive Engagements

Listen up, folks! According to those design geniuses at IDEO, teams that have the freedom to come up with new ideas are a whopping 61 percent more successful than those that are stuck in their old ways. And if that's not enough to convince you, teams that work together and have the right tools to experiment are 32 percent more likely to succeed than those that don't.[1]

But wait, there's more! My team and I have been testing out engagement activities for over a decade now, and let me tell you—they work like a charm. We've tried them out on everyone from healthcare professionals to business people to students, and the success stories just keep rolling in. We love hearing how teams have tailored our activities to fit their own needs.

And we can't forget the most important part—every activity in this book comes with a clear rationale. That means you'll know exactly why you're doing what you're doing, and that can really pump up your motivation and energy levels. Plus, let's be real; who wants to do anything without knowing why they're doing it? So, get ready to have some fun, folks, and let's get those creative juices flowing!

Outline of the Book

The 101 engagements in this book are organized into eight sections:

- **Section One: Sparking Community**—Creating community through group engagement in uncommon experiences
- **Section Two: Igniting a Culture That Emboldens Creativity**—Creating a culture that emboldens creative thinking
- **Section Three: Applied Improv**—Building spontaneity, confidence, and agile thinking for individuals and teams
- **Section Four: Energizing Stokes**—Chasing away the doldrums and mid-afternoon slumps
- **Section Five: Tools for Leading Change**—Bringing out the best in people
- **Section Six: Problem-Solving in 60 Minutes or Less**—Helping teams move, think differently, and collaborate
- **Section Seven: Human-Centered Design with Design-Thinking Tools**—Tools and activities to evoke human-centered thinking and solutions
- **Section Eight: Reflection Tools**—Understanding the role of reflection in learning and transformation
- **Bonus Section Nine: Knock-Their-Socks-Off Presentations**—Creating stellar presentations that keep people talking long after the workshop ends

Leading Cognitive Engagements

Step 1: Choose the appropriate engagement.

Consider your situation and the outcome you want. Then, locate the engagement that best aligns with what's happening in your current situation.

Step 2: Get ready.

Answer the following questions to prepare you and your team for the engagement:

1. What is your deeper purpose of engagement?
2. What materials are needed?
3. How will the room be arranged?
4. How will the group be configured?
5. What will each participant do individually?
6. What time is necessary, and is a timekeeper needed?
7. What type of reflection will enhance the group's experience?

Step 3: Have a ton of fun!

Diving In

Remember, use these engagements as you see fit. Tweak them, rename them, change them—whatever you have to do to make them meaningful and work for you and your teams. The important thing is to have fun, create community—and, by all means, **allow each engagement to illuminate the genius and imagination of every participant.** Finally, keep in mind that there is no learning without reflection. So, allow time to reflect on what the different engagements meant to you and your team. And get ready for some super cool surprises!

As I always say, **we are all creative with leadership potential.** Don't let anyone tell you differently. Embrace that inner creativity and let it SHINE! Now you're ready . . . Let's go inspire creativity!

SECTION ONE:
SPARKING COMMUNITY

Purpose:

Creating community through group engagement in uncommon experiences.

Have you ever noticed it's more fun to do things with others? When we see, hear, or do something within a group, it creates a shared experience that brings us closer together. Not only does this benefit us as individuals, but it also strengthens our group as a whole. In fact, shared experiences can even empower teams to achieve more than they ever thought possible! Even the smallest shared experiences can create a sense of belonging and trust, which is so important for building strong relationships. That's why each of the cognitive engagements in this section is designed to help you connect with others in a meaningful way. These experiences will spark your curiosity, help you grow, and give you a chance to reflect on your thoughts and feelings. And best of all, they'll help you build a sense of community that you can be proud to be a part of!

101 Activities to Ignite Collaboration, Boost Creativity, and Fuel Innovation

Line, Word, and 1 Letter at a Time

Try this to . . . illustrate the power of creative collaboration in a rapid, fun way.

Is your team stuck? Do they need to be more collaborative? Or are you just looking for a fast-paced, fun engagement that illustrates the power of creative collaboration? The quick and simple Line, Word, and Letter at a Time activity might be just the answer.

Benefits

- Pushes participants to think differently and embrace the outcomes
- Gives a sense of accomplishment

Resources Required

- Sharpies or felt pens
- Stopwatch or timer on your phone
- Whiteboard or large piece of paper for each group

How It Works

- Begin by creating groups of four to five people.

- *Round 1:* One person draws a line on the whiteboard or poster. A second team member picks up where the previous team member left off, continuing the line but not creating a new line. Then, a third and forth go, and so on. Continue adding one line at a time to the group's drawing until everyone feels the design is complete.

- *Round 2:* Create a story one word at a time, just like creating the drawing one line at a time. A team member offers up one word. The next team member adds another word, then a third, and so forth until the team believes they have created a story that highlights their artwork.

- *Round 3:* Name the creation one letter at a time. A team member calls out a letter, another group member follows with another letter, and the next team member calls out yet another letter. This cycle continues until the group feels satisfied with the name. Names can get pretty wild.

- *Round 4:* It's show and tell time. Teams take turns sharing their creations.

- *Round 5:* A quick reflection ends the session with the following questions:
  - What meaning can be drawn from this engagement?
  - How did you feel when the activity went in a different direction than you planned?
  - What new learnings might be applied professionally?

101 Activities to Ignite Collaboration, Boost Creativity, and Fuel Innovation

Paired Story

Try this to . . . get a group's creative juices going.

Paired Story provides the opportunity for rapid-fire thinking, open-minded listening, and building on what's happening ("Yes, and . . .").

Benefits

- Ignites creativity within a group

Resources Required

- Bell

How It Works

- *Step 1*: Invite participants to pair up for one round of Paired Story.
- *Step 2*: Call for two random words that will become the subject of the story.
- *Step 3*: The partner with the shortest hair goes first.
- *Step 4*: When the bell rings, each pair begins their story with, "Once upon a time . . ."
- *Step 5*: Each time the bell rings, the person talking stops either mid-sentence or mid-word, and their partner continues the story.
- *Step 6*: Ringing the bell multiple times signals the end of round one.

For the extreme experience, repeat three rounds of Paired Story. Participants grab a new partner, two new words are chosen, and the round begins with the sound of the bell. A brief reflection follows the third round.

Typical Scenario

Richard knew Paired Story could spark a group's energy. He paired up his team, asked for two words, and rang the bell. Within seconds, the room was a buzz of story creation. When Richard rang the bell several times, everyone stopped. Several were eager to share their stories. After a few minutes, Richard ran a quick reflection. He asked the group two questions: what lessons can we learn from Paired Story, and how does Paired Story resemble innovation?

Paper Fusion

Laundry Bicycle

Try this to . . . give your team some fun and practice in idea generation.

Paper Fusion provides a vivid demonstration of how quickly new ideas can be born if people are willing to think differently and put new thoughts into action.

Benefits

- Provides experience in rapid idea generation and concept formation

Resources Required

- Green, eight-by-ten-inch sheets of paper
- Index cards colored pink and yellow
- Pencils
- Tables

How It Works

Divide groups into four or five. Hand each group one stack of 30 pink index cards, one pile of 30 yellow index cards, and a sheet of green, eight-by-ten paper.

- *Step 1:* Team members are given one minute to quickly draw objects on the pink index cards. Only one object per index card. The drawings should be simple objects, such as an apple, a cat, a house, etc. When time is called, all pink index cards are put aside.

- *Step 2:* With one minute on the clock, teams write as many services (such as dentistry, landscaping, or window washing, for example) as they can on the yellow index cards, one per paper. When time is called, all yellow index cards are put aside.

- *Step 3:* Teams create clever, unique, and/or funny combinations between the pink and yellow cards. For example, if someone combined a cat (object from a pink card) and a talent scout (service from the yellow card), it might look like a cat talent agency. Any combination is possible, but each team selects one combination.

- *Step 4:* Teams have five minutes to create imaginary businesses from the combinations they created. Teams use the green sheet to develop the business from the items below. Share this list on the poster, screen, or whiteboard.
  - Business name
  - Product
  - The problem the company solves

- ○ Target audience
- ○ Business model—how money is made
- ○ Slogan
- *Step 5*: Groups share the businesses they created.
- *Step 6*: Groups are asked a reflection question: How might Paper Fusion build skills in idea generation?

Typical Scenario

Enoc, a team guide, wanted to prepare his group for idea generation, so he ran a Paper Fusion.

He divided the group into four teams of five. Then, he gave the instructions and handed out the Paper Fusion cards and papers with pink cards signifying objects, yellow cards signifying services, and green papers signifying business plans. When everyone had their index cards, Enoc called, "Begin." The groups began sketching objects on their pink paper.

Everyone was busy sketching all sorts of objects: bicycles, trees, and umbrellas. After one minute, Enoc called time. Everyone put the pink cards to the side, and Enoc instructed the groups to write as many services as they could think of on the yellow index cards, one service per card. People worked quickly.

At the one-minute mark, Enoc called time. "Now, you will create unusual combinations between the objects (pink cards) and services (yellow cards). Create a business from your mash-ups using the green business plan template to create your business," he instructed. Everyone was engaged. Enoc walked among the groups, reminding them of the time, but most groups didn't seem to hear him as they intently focused on creating their businesses.

After five minutes passed, Enoc called time and invited the groups to share their businesses. Group members eagerly spoke up. Everyone listened, laughed, and expressed amazement at the various ideas.

Enoc asked for a show of hands if people thought a specific business idea was good. In the end, he invited the group to consider how this engagement helped prepare them for ideation generation.

Step Forward Step Back

Try this to . . . demonstrate the discomfort of creative thinking.

There's nothing like getting thrown out of your comfort zone to change your perspective. Step Forward Step Back is designed to do just that. This activity really gets people going!

Benefits

- Raises awareness of personal reactions when encountering the unexpected

How It Works

This is a simple and fast engagement. Begin by asking everyone to stand. Then, ask participants to follow your specific instructions, detailed on the cheat sheet below.

- *Round 1:* "Do what I say, and say what I say."

  The guide says, "Step forward."

  The group steps forward and says, "Step forward."

- *Round 2:* "Do the opposite of what I say, but say what I say."

  The guide says, "Step forward."

  The group steps backward but says, "Step forward."

- *Round 3:* "Do what I say, but say the opposite of what I say."

  The guide says, "Step forward."

  The group steps forward but says, "Step back."

- The guide can also up the confusion by calling out additional instructions like step left, step right, sit down, and stand up—whatever keeps the group moving and guessing.

- A quick reflection after the final round is key to helping participants draw meaning from the engagement. Reflection is simple with the following questions:

  - "What lessons can be drawn from being thrown into a state of confusion?"

  - "What did you notice about yourself when you became confused?"

  - "How might those insights help you professionally or personally?"

- Allow time for processing the questions. People can either think individually and then share or work in pairs to share their insights before sharing with the larger group.

Typical Scenario

Juliana wanted the group to see how creativity takes us out of our comfort zones. So, she introduced Step Forward Step Back. In the first round, everyone followed along perfectly. As Juliana moved to the second round, confusion set in, but it wasn't until the third set of instructions that people broke into laughter, gave up, and applauded their efforts. She asked the group, "What could this engagement teach us about creativity?"

Thirty  Circles

Try this to . . . build creative confidence.

Sometimes, people need a vivid example that demonstrates how they are creative. Thirty Circles is a great way to nudge people to accept their innate creativity.

Benefits

- Leads to a vivid demonstration that everyone is creative

Resources Required

- Thirty Circles worksheets
- Pencils with erasers
- Timer or stopwatch

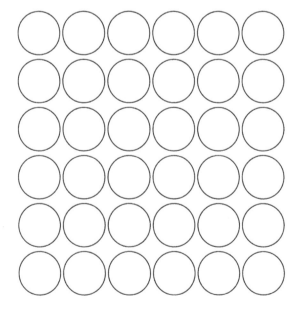

How It Works

Hand out copies of the Thirty Circles worksheet and pencils. Invite participants to transform each circle into a recognizable object in three minutes. Provide an example by filling in a circle with something like a sun or smiling face. Give <u>no other instructions.</u> Simply say, "Go!" Then, start the stopwatch.

Typical Scenario

Nicole felt the Thirty Circles engagement would help her team to stop doubting their creative abilities. She handed out the Thirty Circles sheets and pencils and explained the rules. Someone in the group exclaimed, "I'll never be able to think of 30 different things!"

Another chimed in: "I can't draw." Nicole ignored the comments and encouraged the group to just try and see what happens.

Then, she said, "Ready, set, go!" All over the room, people were bent over the Thirty Circles pages, scribbling out designs. When Nicole called time, there were many comments, such as "Wow, that was fun" and "I got all 30 done just in time." People were excited to share their designs.

When Nicole asked what lessons could be learned, one lady offered, "At first, I couldn't see any way I could sketch 30 things, especially not in three minutes, but I did it!" Everyone spontaneously broke into a cheer.

Nicole smiled and said, "Never doubt your creative ability."

Twisted Thinking

Try this to . . . raise personal awareness.

Twisted Thinking turns the camera back on ourselves, showing how the past drives our thinking and behavior. It also shines a light on blind spots and assumptions that block creative thinking.

Benefits

- Helps identify our thinking patterns

Resources Required

- Notebook or paper
- Pens or pencils

- Retro toys
- Stopwatch

How It Works

Note that the goal of this engagement is to help people see their thoughts and emotional responses when asked to do a specific task and what changes as that task requires them to become more vulnerable. Each participant will be asked to perform in front of the group; however, unbeknownst to the participant, they won't actually perform. Instead, at the guide's directions, they will capture the emotions and thoughts they were experiencing when they thought they were going to perform.

- *Step 1*: Gather a bunch of retro toys—whatever works in your culture—before the session. In the United States, these toys may be yo-yos, jump ropes, pick-up sticks, spinning tops, or jacks, among others. Think of toys that today's adults played with when they were children.

- *Step 2*: Launch the Twisted Thinking engagement by presenting the team with various retro toys. Team members are given a few minutes to preview all the toys but not start playing with any of them yet.

- *Step 3*: After 30 seconds, invite everyone to take one of the toys. Instruct them to pick up their toy, hold it, look at it, and play with it. Then, ask them to pause. Again, have them turn back to their notebooks and capture what they are thinking. Finally, invite everyone to share their reflections.

- *Step 4*: After that, tell them they have two minutes to prepare performances with their toys, which they will perform in front of the group. Give them time to prepare. Just before the performances begin, tell everyone to pause and return to their journals to capture their reactions to performing in front of the group. Give them a few seconds. Invite group members to share their reactions. At this point, many groups will get the lesson of Twisted Thinking. Allow everyone to compare the different responses they had. What might they learn from their personal reactions? How might they apply their responses to their innovation work?

- *Optional*: Some groups may want to go forward with the performances. If so, invite group members to pull their chairs into a circle after the second group shares. Each member performs. Once the performances end, ask everyone to pause, turn back to their notebooks, and capture their thoughts and feelings for one last time. What new ideas did they have? What did this experience show them? How will they apply their new learnings both professionally and personally?

- *Step 5*: For a debrief and reflection, invite the group to share any new insights and learnings the Twisted Thinking experience provided. It's okay if some group members don't want to speak. Encourage everyone to learn from each other.

Typical Scenario

When Cecil, a team guide, noticed the team was stuck, he decided to try Twisted Thinking. He showed the group a large tray of retro toys: wooden yo-yos, spinning tops, jump ropes, jacks, and a host of other toys from days gone by. "Play with them, and then pick your favorite," he instructed.

People instantly exclaimed, "I haven't seen or played jacks in decades!" Everyone perked up as they began playing with the various toys. Lots of laughter ensued.

Cecil gave everyone a few minutes and then said, "Everyone stop. Put the toys down. In your journals, write down the thoughts you had as you interacted with the toys." Team members began writing. After a bit, Cecil called for group members to share. Team members said they enjoyed seeing the toys; the experience took them back to their childhoods.

Then, Cecil invited the group to pick up their favorite toy. Once everyone found a favorite, Cecil gave them a few seconds to play. Then, he announced, "You have two minutes to prepare to perform with your toy in front of the group. Your time starts now." Cecil started the timer. The team immediately became serious, and Cecil encouraged everyone to get ready to perform.

After two minutes, Cecil called time. "Everyone, go back to your journals, and write down your thoughts and feelings when you heard you were going to have to perform for the group." After a few minutes, Cecil called for group members to share what they wrote. It was clear: everyone's comments had changed from their first journal entries! The words went from happy to frustrated, scared, and doubtful.

People were surprised at how quickly the experience went from one of fun to dread and fear. As they continued reflecting, the group expressed appreciation to Cecil for guiding them through Twisted Thinking and raising their awareness. Some said it was the first time they slowed down to take stock of their thinking and self-talk. One member said, "I usually just react." Some of the group said they wanted to try Twisted Thinking in other settings.

Then, someone asked, "When do we perform?"

Cecil said, "Now, if anyone wants to." A few people stepped up and showed off their prowess with their toys, sparking lots of laughter and great comments. In the end, Cecil felt the engagement was a success.

SECTION TWO:
IGNITING
a Culture
that
Emboldens
CREATIVITY

Purpose:

Creating a culture that
emboldens creative thinking.

We all pretty much know the huge role culture plays in shaping our identity and how we behave. It's true! Sometimes, it can be a good thing, but other times, it can be a bit of a challenge. Wouldn't it be great if we could all work in a culture that encourages creativity, trust, and forgiveness? Well, the good news is that it's possible! Even if your current company culture isn't quite there yet, you can take steps to create a more collaborative and innovative environment. As a leader or team member, there are certain skills and tools you can develop to help foster a culture that supports creativity and innovation. We've put together some activities that can help you get started on building the kind of culture you want to work in!

The Badge Tree

Try this to . . . provide a dynamic symbol for collaboration and co-creation.

The Badge Tree is an artifact and a ritual that gives everyone a voice and the opportunity to move beyond hierarchical structures, even for a short time. The Badge Tree is a constant reminder that we all have a voice!

Benefits

- Creates a way to discuss hierarchy and how it can block creativity

Resources Required

- An artifact that resembles a tree

How It Works

The Badge Tree can be anything from an artificial plant to an actual small tree. The tree is designed to be used for groups consisting of people from all levels of the organization or the community. At the start of a meeting or project, the guide introduces the Badge Tree as an overt symbol that everyone has a voice and the permission and responsibility to use it. Then, the guide invites everyone to hang their work badges on the tree. As people attach their badges to the tree, they say, "Checking in."

Typical Scenario

Lou was leading a project that consisted of people from all levels of the company and from a variety of backgrounds. She knew the Badge Tree would come in handy with this group. Once everyone was in the room, Lou pointed to the Badge Tree and explained, "Meet the Badge Tree. It's an overt symbol and a vivid reminder of the equity we believe in. It means voices from everywhere and ideas from everyone." She went on to say, "Everyone has permission to be on this project and the responsibility to acknowledge the inclusiveness that the Badge Tree represents." She then invited everyone to hang their badges on the Badge Tree. Some loved this whole idea while others were not quite so sure.

Find badge.   *Take off badge.*   *Hang on tree.*

Forget badge.   *Remember badge.*

Lou sensed skepticism among the group, so she asked Wayne, a group member who had previous experience with the Badge Tree, to share his thoughts. "All of us are here on this project to solve a difficult challenge. The Badge Tree reminds us to work collaboratively and that we all have an equal voice," he said.

The Badge Tree became a potent symbol of openness, safe spaces, equality, and collaboration at the innovation lab and helped the group create a beautiful ritual far beyond anything they ever envisioned.

The Campfire Table

Try this to . . . create a place for informal yet meaningful conversations.

Most conference or board rooms are not designed for real conversation. Too many times, the only option is the long, rectangular boardroom table, the antithesis of informal conversation. The Campfire Table may be your answer to this problem.

Benefits

- Provides a relaxed setting for important yet informal conversations

Resources Required

- Informal chairs
- Low, round table or something that can simulate a campfire setting
- Snacks

How It Works

Since the Campfire Table is both low and round, it feels like gathering around a campfire, which sets an inclusive, informal tone that builds community. Low, informal chairs around the Campfire Table helps everyone feel included and visible. Eye contact is easier, enabling those who might be less engaged to speak up. Finally, the Campfire Table puts snacks within everyone's reach!

Typical Scenario

Ben's team wasn't sure the Campfire Table was a good idea. After all, everyone would be sitting on low folding chairs. They were used to comfy, leather chairs with the leader seated at the end of a long table. However, it didn't take long for everyone to realize that, with the Campfire Table, conversations were easier and more fun, and a sense of community emerged. Despite the diverse nature of the groups who used the campfire table, everyone there—from top leadership to the front-line workers—felt visible.

Compliment Cake

Try this to . . . celebrate team members' birthdays in a clever way.

Office birthdays can be challenging. Deb gets a cake, Dave gets a birthday gram, and Cheryl's birthday is forgotten. Kim is saving for a car and resents chipping in for some cheesy gift. Every office needs a birthday strategy. The Compliment Cake may be the answer. Birthdays never need to be a burden again.

Benefits

- Provides a simple, fun way to honor team members on their birthdays

Resources Required

- Hat or another object that resembles a cake

How It Works

On a team member's birthday, get out the Compliment Cake hat, and place it on the birthday person's head. Team members gather around in a circle with the birthday person in the middle. Everyone takes turns sharing one thing they've appreciated about the birthday person in the past year. The Compliment Cake hat isn't fancy. A cheap party hat from Party City will do the trick. The key is not the hat itself but what it represents. And who doesn't want to hear how much others appreciate them?

Typical Scenario

It was Jill's birthday. Patrick, the Compliment Cake monitor, let everyone know to gather after lunch for Jill's Compliment Cake bash. At the time, a team member brought Jill into the room. Patrick brought in the hat and placed it on Jill's head, and team members shared what they appreciated about Jill that year. Even though the Compliment Cake felt a little awkward at first, everyone voted to make it an office tradition.

Goal Pose

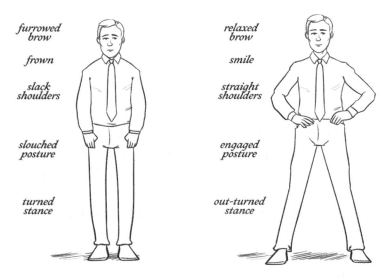

furrowed brow	*relaxed brow*
frown	*smile*
slack shoulders	*straight shoulders*
slouched posture	*engaged posture*
turned stance	*out-turned stance*

Try this to . . . share nonverbal feelings about an assignment, project, or event.

When teams face a challenge or are in the throes of a big project, emotions can run high and often go unarticulated. The Goal Pose helps capture the team's feelings in those times. It's a cool way to document growth and change through a project's journey.

Benefits

- Captures a team's transformation and growth during a project

Resources Required

- Camera or phone for taking pictures of team members' poses
- Copy machine
- Bulletin board

How It Works

At the beginning and end of a project, each team member is photographed. Each person strikes a pose that represents their emotion about the project. Once all photographs are taken, photocopies are made, and the copies are hung on a wall or bulletin board. Team members share the meaning behind their photographs. The photographs remain on the bulletin board or wall for the duration of the project and become a part of the team's journey.

At the close of the project, a second photo is taken that captures team members' feelings now that the project is completed. Once all team members are photographed, they are copied and hung beside the first photograph. Team members share the meaning behind their second photographs, how the two photographs are different, and why it matters. All team members are given the opportunity to share. If the group is too large, the share-out could be held in two sessions.

Typical Scenario

Ramya felt nervous about her department's project. She was afraid that the project would fail and that their team would look silly. In her first photograph, Ramya struck a pose with her hands covering her face. The rest of the team was photographed, and soon, photocopies of the team's poses hung on the office bulletin board. At the next team meeting, members shared the meaning behind their own photographs. The comments were enlightening and helped the team understand each other. The photographs became part of each team meeting for the duration of the project.

At the end of the project, everyone took a second photograph. This photo captured their feelings now that the project was completed. Again, photographs were copied and brought to the team meeting. Each team member hung their two photographs side by side. A meeting was scheduled for each team member to share the meaning of their second pose and how it contrasted with the first. In the end, the director asked the team if this engagement was helpful. The team felt the process created meaningful conversations and made it easier to share their feelings about the project accurately. The director shared that, even though feeling can't drive a product, the Goal Pose created better team spirit, which improved the project outcome.

Try this to . . . ensure all team members' thoughts, ideas, and feelings are being heard.

New insights and learnings often get lost in the energy of "bigger" ideas or "flashier" prototypes. The Insight Infusion ensures new learnings are heard.

Benefits

- Provides a way for team members to share new insights and ideas that might otherwise not be shared

Resources Required

- Team members willing to speak up

How It Works

As a team works on a challenge, it records, captures, and focuses on information that seems relevant. Sometimes, seemingly unrelated insights, learnings, or insights get overlooked. This means vital information gets lost. To ensure this doesn't happen, any team member can call for an Insight Infusion. To do this, the team stands in a circle while the person who called the Insight Infusion shares important pieces of information. The team gives a quick response and decides if something different needs to be done.

Typical Scenario

Trevor's group felt the team had rushed and that some vital information was being disregarded. So, he called for an Insight Infusion. The group gathered in a standing circle. The new information was shared. Trevor then called for the team to decide if the new information should be considered. If the team said yes, they would decide on the next steps. If the team believed the information would not improve the project's outcome, they would return to work as usual. In any case, Insight Infusion gives everyone a voice and creates a safety net for any project.

Joke Night

Try this to . . . give your team something completely different.

You and your team need a break, a change of pace, and a way to see each other in a new light. Setting time for a good laugh is one way to shake things up. Enter Joke Night.

Benefits

- Fosters team spirit and fun

Resources Required

- Joke master/emcee (can either be a volunteer or assigned position)
- Refreshments
- Silly, cheap prize

How It Works

A team decides on a good time for Joke Night. The team votes on a goofy prize for the best and worst jokes. We've used a wooden spoon for the worst joke and a purple scarf for the best joke, but the prizes can be anything! Each team member comes with one joke and one humorous anecdote to share.

After a few minutes of chatting and snacking, the joke master calls the official start of Joke Night. Anyone can start, and the group continues telling jokes in popcorn style. Each team member tells their joke while the audience cheers or groans. The joke master keeps things moving and records who gets the biggest laughs and loudest boos. Once the team is joked out, the Joke Master announces the winner and loser and hands out the prizes. Prizes are only held by the winner and loser until the next Joke Night.

Mantra Moments

Try this to . . . capture the wisdom within your group.

Teams are intelligent and full of wisdom, yet it's easy for this wisdom to go unnoticed or unrecognized. Most leaders need a way to capture a team's brilliant ideas, moments of inspiration, or funny little quips. Mantra Moments is designed to bring those important tidbits to life and get their proper dues.

Benefits

- Showcases your team's wisdom and builds an organic library of wise soundbites

Resources Required

- Something to write on
- Writing utensil

How It Works

When a team member says something worth remembering, it is captured on a blank poster designated for the Mantra Moments. The mantras are posted around the room for all to see. A few minutes are set aside during weekly department meetings to celebrate any new mantras.

Typical Scenario

During a team project, Nancy, a team member, exclaimed, "We are moving too fast! Why don't we slow down to learn faster?"

Another team member, Paul, heard Nancy and called out, "What a great reminder!" He didn't waste a moment, writing Nancy's words on a large Post-it Note and sticking it on the Mantra Moments wall. As the team progressed through its project, Nancy's statement was a good reminder to slow down. When the project ended, Nancy's mantra wasn't the only one that hung on the wall; other team members' wise words were also there.

At the next department meeting, the team reviewed the new mantras, and someone said, "Wow, we've got a wise team!"

Try this to . . . reframe difficult or embarrassing situations.

There's an old adage: "The crisis of today is the joke of tomorrow." It's true, and remembering it can help you manage disruption when it hits. Resurrecting Embarrassment gives you the opportunity to reframe an embarrassing situation in order to build the resilience that creativity demands.

Benefits

- Shows us how to stop taking ourselves too seriously

Resources Required

- A few minutes of everyone's time
- People willing to share an embarrassing experience

How It Works

Each team member recalls embarrassing moments. Then, one by one, the moments are shared. A quick Q&A follows each story. The person sharing can offer up lessons learned from the experience. Since everyone is sharing embarrassing moments, a community emerges, and laughs are shared—not just at each other's expense but as a team. By the time everyone has finished, the team is ready for honest conversation and trust building.

Typical Scenario

When Sunita's team gathered for Resurrecting Embarrassment, one team member began with a funny story. Then, people responded with laughter and empathy as each team member told their embarrassing experience. Sunita finally described how her suitcase split open as she ran for a plane. Everything flew everywhere—including the forbidden, Italian-made Kinder Eggs she had snuck through U.S. customs. Everyone enjoyed Sunita's story; others felt emboldened to share their red-faced tales. This engagement always evokes lots of fun, laughter, and personal connection.

Try this to . . . demystify the creative process.

When problem-solving or working on complex projects, we need specific roles that serve as reminders to be creative and venture into new territories. The Magic Sauce makes that possible.

Benefits

- Creates easy ways to embrace creativity while helping others do the same

Resources Required

- Round, two-to-three-inch stickers that are red, green, and yellow
- Sharpies

How It Works

At the onset of a project or meeting, the leader introduces the Magic Sauce of Creativity:

- Embrace your innate creativity (green)
- Suspend negative judgment (red)
- Be curious, observe, and question (yellow)

Once introduced, the leader invites members to choose one of the Magic Sauce elements to champion. A stack of colored, round stickers (green, red, and yellow) is placed on the table. Each sticker represents one of the Magic Sauce elements. Team members choose a sticker representing a Magic Sauce component. Once selected, each person draws a quick sketch representing that Magic Sauce element. For example, "be curious, observe, and question" could be a question mark or two eyes. People can get creative. Each team member sticks the sticker on their shirts, coats, or somewhere visible so others can see. That person is then the advocate for that element of the Magic Sauce.

In other words, each member chooses the Magic Sauce element they promise to keep alive throughout the project. If there are multiple small groups or subgroups, all components of the Magic Sauce must be represented in each group. Each component can be represented by more than one team member.

Shirkers, Clean Freaks, and Nerds

Try this to . . . engage your team and keep your workspace clean.

In today's age of budget cuts, employees are mandated to do more with less. This often means that mundane chores fall on team members' shoulders—tasks like emptying the trash, vacuuming, and (the horror of horrors) cleaning the bathroom. Not everyone willingly grabs a mop or a toilet brush. Too often, such tasks repeatedly fall on one or two willing souls. This is where Shirkers, Clean Freaks, and Nerds (SCF&N) provides a way for everyone to pitch in!

Benefits

- Removes stigma while creating a sense of community about taking care of the team's space

Resources Required

- Cleaning supplies
- Bulletin board for posting weekly zones to clean

How It Works

Divide team members into groups, and instruct them to choose wacky team names (which is how we came up with the name "Shirkers, Clean Freaks, and Nerds"). The team decides what tasks are needed for each area to be cleaned, i.e. bathrooms, breakroom, etc. Every Monday, each group chooses a different zone to clean. That way, chores are shared, and no one gets stuck doing the same task.

Typical Scenario

When department lead Liam received the news that environmental services were being cut back, he decided to give Shirkers, Clean Freaks, and Nerds a try. At first, no one was interested, but Liam didn't give up and called everyone to brainstorm how to make the chores fun. Soon enough, everyone joined in, and people began to see the value of communal cleanliness. Their spirits lifted, and the space stayed a lot cleaner.

Show-Off Seat

Try this to . . . honor a team member's accomplishment.

The Show-Off Seat is a two-way win. It provides an opportunity for co-workers to notice and celebrate each other's good work while giving team members a chance to share their accomplishments in a quick, energetic way. The Show-Off Seat keeps the busyness of work from obscuring the value of a team member's contributions.

Benefits

- Honors a specific team member's accomplishment in a quick, fun way

Resources Required

- Stool
- Stopwatch or timer

How It Works

A chair or stool is designated as the Show-Off Seat and becomes the team's celebratory artifact. The conditions for the Show-Off Seat are:

- Anyone can call a Show-Off Seat moment; they become the host.
- The Show-Off Seat moment lasts for four minutes.
  - In the first two minutes, the Show-Off Seat honoree shares what they did, why it mattered, and what they liked about the experience.
  - In the last two minutes, the team members offer praise for the honoree's accomplishment.
- The Show-Off Seat moment is called when someone notices a team member has done something noteworthy, major or minor.
- The host sets a time for the Show-Off Seat and invites the team. At the prearranged time, everyone gathers around the honoree who sits on the Show-Off Seat. The host gives a quick introduction, invites the honoree to share, and starts the timer. The honoree gives the highlights of their accomplishment and why it mattered. At two minutes, the host calls for time and invites team members to share what they liked or praise the honoree. A quick Q&A can follow if needed. Everyone is thanked for attending.

Typical Scenario

Sharon put a presentation together that won over a big group. Her presentation was excellent and funny, and it moved the company forward. When Sharon returned to her team, Jill called for a Show-Off Seat. Jill asked someone to grab a stool and invited Sharon to sit. Jill gave a quick introduction to why Sharon was being celebrated and started the stopwatch, and Sharon shared the highlights of her presentation. After two minutes passed, Jill then invited team members to call for a quick Q&A. Jill led the group in the final round of clapping.

Sharon responded by saying, "This was wonderful. Thanks for listening, and I can't wait to honor someone else this way." As the Show-Off Seat became part of the team culture, several team members felt a deeper sense of community developing.

Try this to . . . deepen your team's understanding of each other.

Everyone wants to work on a high-functioning team and feel fulfilled at work. However, hierarchical structures and work demands can keep that from happening. The This Is How I Roll engagement provides a way to better understand teammates and see them through their strengths.

Benefits

- Builds understanding of team members' preferences and idiosyncrasies

Resources Required

- Room with a space big enough for people to move around
- Four large posters

How It Works

- *Step 1:* Create four signs that say:
  - *North:* Acting—likes to act, try things, and plunge in.
  - *East:* Speculating—looks at the big picture and the possibilities before acting.
  - *South:* Caring—likes to consider everyone's feelings and voices before acting.
  - *West:* Detail—likes to know who, what, when, where, and why before acting.
- *Step 2:* Hang up the posters in the four corners of the room.
- *Step 3:* Everyone stands by the poster that accurately captures their work preference. Once everyone has decided, ask participants to observe who has ended up in each group.
- *Step 4:* Ask each team to select individuals for the following roles:
  - Recorder—records responses of the group.
  - Timekeeper—keeps the group members on task.
  - Spokesperson—shares on behalf of the group when the time is called.
- *Step 5:* Once selected, each team member will have five to eight minutes to respond to the following questions:
  - What are the strengths of your style? (3-4 adjectives)
  - What are the limitations of your style? (3-4 adjectives)

- What style do you find most challenging and why?
- What do people from other "directions" or styles need to know about you, so you can effectively work together?
- What's one thing you value about each of the other three styles?

- *Step 6*: The activity ends with a quick reflection on this simple question: In what ways did this engagement increase your awareness of yourself and other team members?

Typical Scenario

Nicole felt her team didn't understand one another. This was hindering their work, so she introduced them to This Is How I Roll. She hung up the four posters, one in each corner of the room according to the proper orientation. So, the north poster hung in the northern corner, the south poster hung in the southern corner, and so forth. She invited the team members to read each poster then stand under the poster that best reflected each person. The team took a moment to read the different posters. People moved to the poster they felt best aligned with their strengths. Once everyone had chosen a corner, Nicole asked the different groups to share the reasons they chose a specific poster. After about 10 minutes, Nicole asked the group to share. Nicole wasn't sure people would be willing to share, but people jumped in. She was pleasantly surprised. Team members expressed an appreciation for the opportunity to better understand each other.

Wisdom Wednesday (WW)

Try this to . . . create community across the organization.

Everyone wants to work in a place where community thrives. Wisdom Wednesdays helps make that possible. It's a fun, interactive, weekly lunch where team members share accomplishments, new learnings, or high-interest stories. Each Wisdom Wednesday goal is to stimulate the mind and build community.

Benefits

- Builds community among departments and with everyone within the organization

Resources Required

- Host
- Speaker
- Simple lunch items (or participants bring their own lunches)

How It Works

Wisdom Wednesdays (WW) is a 30-minute event, open to the whole organization, where either lunch is provided or participants bring their own lunches. A host introduces a fellow employee who gives a 10-minute presentation. The host leads a Q&A following the presentation.

Typical Scenario

When healthcare employees worked with a medical supply company to save time and money and transform one aspect of surgery, that became a perfect topic for Wisdom Wednesday. So, those employees were invited to be featured at a Wisdom Wednesday. Everyone was inspired by their story. On other Wisdom Wednesdays, presentations were given on simple topics, such as one department's idea to cut down on meetings. The point is to provide a platform for employees to share and promote fellowship.

Woohoo Cheer

Try this to . . . celebrate a brilliant idea in a quick way.

It's easy for a team member's clever idea, insightful thought, or hard work to go unnoticed and not be celebrated. These moments of inspiration just slip away. The Woohoo Cheer solves this problem in a fun, memorable way and also pairs very well with Mantra Moments.

Benefits

- Builds spirit and gives people permission for micro-celebrations

Resources Required

- Team cheer

How It Works

Every team needs unique ways to acknowledge the feedback or insights team members make. The Woohoo Cheer does this with fun and style. It's simple. Any group can create a team cheer by choosing a sound and action that, when combined, makes their cheer. For example, a clap can be accompanied by an exclamation like, "Yeah!" It's a simple, rapid-fire way to acknowledge that something significant has happened.

The rule of the Woohoo cheer is simple. Once someone starts the cheer, everybody must join in. No one can opt out. Anytime someone feels inspired by what someone said, they can initiate the cheer. Cheers are fun and become *big* culture builders for any team.

Typical Scenario

Adriana heard her teammate, Joyce, say, "This is the first time we've truly understood this problem." Her words inspired Adriana, so she enthusiastically clapped. Others joined in and shouted, "Yeah!" In so doing, everyone acknowledged the power of this inspirational point. Adriana and the team laughed and paused to ponder the cheer's significance.

Section Three:

(YES AND!)

APPLIED IMPROV

Purpose:
Building sponaneity, confidence, and agile thinking for individuals and teams.

SAY Yes, and

Sometimes, we just need to let loose and laugh. This is exactly what classic improv does for a group. The activities included in this section are fun and fast and require participants to be present and fully engaged. Plus, improv is all about good listening and intentional responses, which we could all use a bit more of in our lives. This section is filled with all sorts of engaging activities that will help bring your group closer together and provide lots of opportunities for learning and reflection. So, let's just relax, have some fun, and let go of all our worries! In addition, improv demands good listening and intentional responses—just what we all need. This section offers a host of engagements that create bonds and provide rich opportunities for learning and reflection. Let go and have fun!

Be a Square

Try this to . . . jump-start a project or help a team get unstuck.

There are many reasons why teams get stuck. Whatever the reason, a shift in attention can often get the team moving. Be A Square may be just the ticket.

Benefits

- Builds trust, listening, and collaboration

Resources Required

- Blindfolds (one for each participant)
- Empty room
- Long rope

How It Works

Place a rope on the floor that runs along the room's length. Ask each participant to blindfold themselves and spin in a circle a few times. Then, the team works together to transform the perfectly straight rope into a square.

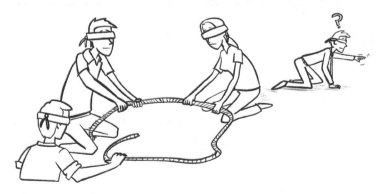

Try this to . . . build connections and empathy among team members.

Employees often make incorrect assumptions about what is happening in their departments. Commonalities bring people together either face to face or in video chat rooms to create more cohesive teams.

Benefits

- Helps team members find commonalities

Resources Required

- Elevator music to welcome teams back from breakout rooms
- Timer

How It Works

The leader divides everybody into groups and places them in a virtual or real breakout room. Each group has three minutes to discover and document the things they have in common. At the end of the three minutes, everyone comes back together. Each group reads its list of commonalities. Any commonality that is the same as another team is crossed off everyone's lists. The group with the most unique things in common "wins."

Typical Scenario

Andy's virtual group needed something to boost its energy. So, he introduced Commonalities, gave the instructions, sent each team to different locations to find commonalities, and started the timer.

All four teams rushed for the next three minutes to find common ground. Team One discovered seven commonalities while Team Two and Team Four came up with 10 commonalities. When the time was up, Andy brought everyone back to the general virtual space.

"We tied!" Bob and Lucy shouted.

"Maybe you did," Andy said, "but if another group has the same commonality, it doesn't count."

Lucy, from Team One, read each of her team's commonalities, things like "I own a Toyota," "I have relatives in Arkansas," and "I hate strawberry ice cream." Neither of the other two teams had any of those.

But when Bob from Team Two read his list, the first one he mentioned, "I've been to both Disneyland and Disney World," immediately prompted Jim from Team Four, who said, "Hey, we also had that one!"

Everyone laughed, and Andy said, "Well, that makes it official. Not only do we have a lot of Disney fans, but Team One wins with the most unique commonalities. Congratulations!" When the office meeting resumed, the team was more engaged.

Dance for Dancing's Sake

Try this to . . . break up the monotony of a long or boring meeting.

Meetings, meetings, meetings fill our days. It doesn't take a rocket scientist to know that meetings drain people. That's where Dance for Dancing's Sake comes in. It's a zany, unconventional way to break up long meetings or even to kick off a meeting.

Benefits
- Raises energy

Resources Required
- Music playlist
- Timekeeper
- Scribe to record eliminated dance moves
- A Dr. Doldrum
- Timer

How It Works

Someone is assigned to be Dr. Doldrum, who hates to smile or dance. The goal is to get Dr. Doldrum to do either or both. Each time the pair fails to make Dr. Doldrum smile or dance, the dance move they used is eradicated. That move can not be used or repeated by another group or team member.

- *Step 1*: On small pieces of paper, write each participant's name and place them in a bowl.

- *Step 2*: Dr. Doldrum draws two pieces of paper from the bowl and calls out the names.

- *Step 3*: Those two people have 20 seconds to co-create a dance. At time, Dr. Doldrum starts the music, and the pair must do their dance for 30 seconds.

- *Step 4*: If Dr. Doldrum hasn't joined in the dance or smiled after 30 seconds, Dr. Doldrum eliminates one of the pair's dance moves. On the other hand, if Dr. Doldrum smiles or dances, the couple gets applause, and for 30 seconds, everyone joins in the new dance the pair just created. The pair moves to round two.

- *Step 5*: Then, two other names are drawn. The pair repeats the same 20 seconds to co-create a dance, but this time, if a dance move has been eliminated, they cannot use that move. If the group uses the eliminated dance move, they are out, or if Dr. Doldrum does not smile or dance, the pair is also out. However, if Dr. Doldrum smiles or moves, everyone claps and joins the pair's dance for the next 30 seconds.

- *Step 6*: The process continues. When a pair fails to make Dr. Doldrum smile or move, they receive a strike, and Dr. Doldrum eliminates another move.

- *Step 7*: Once every name has been called and each participant has danced, the pairs that are still in the game have a play-off. They can not use any eliminated moves.

- *Step 8*: This time, instead of dancing for Dr. Doldrum, the pair dances for the rest of the group. After each pair demonstrates their 30-second dance, the group either cheers or boos. Either a winner or a tie is called, and everyone claps.

- *Step 9*: Now, the facilitator invites the participants to pair off and find lessons that can be drawn from this engagement. The following questions might be helpful:
  - What value did this engagement give the team?
  - If you were to lead this engagement, what changes would you make?

- *Step 10*: The facilitator then calls for a few comments from the participants.

With apologies to famous artists.

Try this to . . . build team spirit and deepen bonds.

People want dynamic work environments where conversation is easy and collaboration is the norm. The Puzzle Me This engagement makes this happen.

Benefits

- Illustrates the real cost of invisible barriers that exist in a siloed culture

Resources Required

- Felt pens
- Large pieces of paper (one for each participant)
- Printout of a famous painting (i.e. *Mona Lisa, The Starry Night, The Last Supper*, etc.)
- Scissors

How It Works

Prior to the activity, the facilitator prints a famous, well-known picture and cuts it into as many pieces as there are group members. Each participant takes a puzzle piece, a marker, scissors, and one of the large pieces of paper. Everyone is instructed to create a copy of their puzzle piece—except they must make their drawing five times larger than the original. Each team member gets three to five minutes to complete their picture. When the facilitator calls time, the group comes back together and attempts to put the picture together. After completing the puzzle, the group leader leads everyone through a reflection.

"What can we learn?

"What does this mean?"

"What can we apply to our team or work?"

Typical Scenario

David led a group that admitted they were locked in deep silos. One day, he handed everyone a puzzle piece and gave instructions for each person to recreate their puzzle piece on a large poster board paper that he had provided. Then, team members went to work. There was a lot of chatter and laughter as the group drew, cut, and tried to reproduce their puzzle pieces.

Once the parts were together, David asked the group to reflect on what they had just experienced. He explained that there were many lessons that could be drawn from this engagement, and he was eager to hear what the group learned. He invited everyone to find a quiet spot and silently consider these questions: "What are three insights and/or new learnings you can draw from this engagement that can be applied to your organization? Then, how might those new learnings help you move beyond your habitual ways of thinking and acting?"

David then said, "You will each be asked to share one thing you gained and how you will apply it to your work." He then asked everyone to put their phones aside while they pondered the question.

David gave the group a good ten minutes to mull over the questions. When the bell sounded, he called everyone back to the center and said, "I am eager to hear what you might have learned. Who wants to go first?" David invited the group to write down their insights and create the next steps for collaboration. He also asked the group to think specifically about how members might break down the silos they had identified.

101 Activities to Ignite Collaboration, Boost Creativity, and Fuel Innovation

Super Short Story Challenge

Try this to . . . shake things up.

This is a great engagement when your energy is waning and the conversation stalls. The Super Short Story Challenge invokes curiosity, boosts energy, and builds participants' respect for one another.

Benefits

- Demonstrates how creativity loves constraints

How It Works

We took inspiration from the legend of Ernest Hemingway's six-word story, "Baby shoes for sale, never worn." You can write a story like Hemingway or use simple drawings or motifs to create simple stories. To add to the fun, you can invite your clients to join you.

Typical Scenario

We asked participants to describe their COVID-19 experience by drawing a six-frame cartoon featuring stickmen. Here's what they came up with:

The Expert

Try this to . . . get people to share their thoughts and feelings.

Sometimes, individuals withhold their opinions or questions because they doubt they know enough about the subject matter. The Expert helps participants feel comfortable when speaking up.

Benefits

- Encourages participants to add their ideas to the discussion

Resources Required

- Light background music
- Timer
- Virtual meeting platform

How It Works

Someone is deemed the "expert." The group picks a subject for the expert. This can be anything from skydiving to exotic fish. The less the expert knows about the subject, the more fun the activity. Participants then act like they're attending a conference where the expert is answering questions. The expert must answer questions with great confidence. After two minutes, they designate a new expert, choose a new topic, and go for another two minutes.

Afterward, the facilitator leads a reflection, asking participants about their favorite expert responses or what learnings can be drawn from the exercise. End the reflection by asking participants what tweaks could make the engagement even more meaningful.

You Animal

Try this to . . . infuse some good mo-jo into your team.

Sometimes, innovation team members need a fun, non-threatening way to get to know each other. You Animal can help participants lower their inhibitions and build trust.

Benefits

- Fosters understanding among team members

Resources Required

- Bell
- Board or large Post-it Note
- Sharpies

How It Works

Team members are given one minute to choose an animal that best represents their inner being. A quick Google search is allowed.

Once everyone has chosen, team members take turns revealing their animals by sketching them on a large Post-it Note or whiteboard. The rest of the team members guess the animal. Once the animal is identified, the presenter shares why they chose it.

Typical Scenario

Bridget led a group that had never worked together before. She wanted her group to become better acquainted in a quick, fun way. She explained that everyone had one minute to choose an animal that relates to their personality. Members pulled out their phones and started googling animals and what each represented. Some compared notes, told jokes, and poked fun at each other. Everyone looked engaged.

After two minutes, Bridget asked, "Who wants to share first?"

Richard immediately raised his hand. "Sometimes, I'm told that I'm very independent," he said. "I love the independence and sleekness of horses, so I chose a horse."

Lance went next: "Mine is an eagle because they never eat dead meat. I'm inspired by that because I like to stay focused on the future and not stuck in the past with old, dead problems."

Mary then spoke up. "I chose the lynx because they are solitary creatures that have excellent eyesight. This allows them to spot trouble or problems far away. I relate to this because I love working alone and focusing on the details."

As more and more group members spoke, more laughter and conversation took place. When the activity ended, several participants commented that they enjoyed hearing what animal each person chose and why they chose it. The group felt more connected, and the energy level increased.

SECTION FOUR:

Energizing STOKES

Purpose:

Chasing away the doldrums and mid-afternoon slumps.

I've come to realize that life just gets better when we stop taking ourselves too seriously. I truly mean it! Don't believe me? Give it a shot and see for yourself! Now, I'm not saying we should act irresponsibly, but rather that we should take our work seriously while still being able to laugh at ourselves. That's where these engagement activities come in—they're quick and easy ways to help groups do just that!

Not only are these activities fun, but they also give us a chance to reflect on ourselves in a lighthearted yet meaningful way. While all of the activities in this book will accomplish this goal, the ones in this section are particularly quick and effective. Trust me, just a few minutes is all it takes to shift a group's focus and have some fun!

These activities are perfect for groups of any size and most environments, and they are followed by a quick reflection period. To make sure everyone feels comfortable participating, let them know it's a "no shame, no blame zone," and explain why they're being invited to take part. So, let's have some fun and get ready to laugh!

101 Activities to Ignite Collaboration, Boost Creativity, and Fuel Innovation

Try this to . . . encourage team members to see with new eyes.

How It Works

- *Step 1*: Players stand in a circle. The first player says a word that is related to the team's specific challenge, opportunity, event, etc. For example, this could be planning the Christmas party, launching a new service, or welcoming a new team member.

- *Step 2*: The first player offers up a word all team members relate to. The first word might be "remodel," referring to the remodel the office is undergoing. Another first word could be "sales," relating to the team's current sales campaign. The first word is just a starting point. Where it goes from there is anyone's guess.

- *Step 3*: The second player repeats the first word and adds a second related word that makes a word connection.

- *Step 4*: The third person continues by adding a new word that connects to the previous word. Each new word does not have to connect to the original word. Remember, the idea is *not* to make sentences. Instead, the group focuses only on connecting the word before theirs. For example: dog, dog *bone*, dog bone *fracture*, dog bone fractured leg.

- *Step 5*: Players continue around the circle until everyone has contributed. Then, the entire circle attempts to repeat the previously linked words, forming one long verbal chain. Now, the group has two minutes to go back to the original word and see how different words in the word chain can relate to the first word. Encourage members to stretch their thinking.

- *Step 6*: A quick reflection to wrap up this engagement is very helpful. There is much to debrief about the connections group members made. Some possible considerations are:
  - What new ideas come from the connections?
  - What connections would be interesting to explore?
  - What new insights bubble up as the group debriefs?

Try this to . . . raise energy levels and commitment.

How It Works

Players stand in a circle with one player in the middle. The player in the middle points at someone in the circle and shouts, "Bang!" That player ducks as players to the right and left immediately turn in to face off. Whichever player shoots faster wins the draw, eliminating the other. If the ducking player gets caught in the crossfire, that player is eliminated. When the game gets down to two players, choose a caller. Then, the remaining two players stand back to back and must take a step until the caller says to turn and shoot. The caller may stipulate that the players may not turn until a certain word or another agreed-upon signal is spoken aloud.

30

Try this to . . . raise energy levels and focus.

How It Works

Everyone stands in a circle. One person makes eye contact with someone across the circle. The first person takes a small step forward, claps, and points, saying, "Bing." They then step back into place. The person who received the bing then makes eye contact with another person, steps, claps, and points, while saying, "Bang." Again, they then step back into place. The person receiving the bang then makes eye contact with another person, steps, claps, and points while saying, "Boom." The pattern continues until the pattern gets off track. All players cheer and celebrate and play the next round faster than before.

Mini Activity: Bippity-Bippity-Bop

Try this to . . . raise energy levels and focus.

How It Works

Players stand in a circle with one player in the middle. The person in the middle tries to get replaced by pointing at someone. If someone in the circle doesn't correctly execute things, the person in the center calls them out, and they switch places.

For example, say the person in the center points to someone in the circle and shouts, "Bibbity-bibbity-bop!" So, before the person in the center gets to the end of the phrase, the selected person must say, "Bop!" However, the target must remain silent if the center person only says, "Bop." If the selected person gives a vocal response, that person replaces the person in the center.

The phrase "bibbity-bibbity-bop" can be changed. Allow the group to come up with new phrases.

Mini Activity: Crazy Eights

Try this to . . . get a team up and moving.

1. Shake left arm.   *2. Shake right arm.*   *3. Shake left leg.*   *4. Shake right leg.*

5. Repeat each of above (8 times, then 7 times, etc.) reducing by one each round.

How It Works

The guide invites everyone to stand up, mimic their actions, and count with them.

1. "Raise your right arm, shake your hand, and count: one, two, three, four, five, six, seven, eight."
2. "Raise your left arm, shake your hand, and count: one, two, three, four, five, six, seven."
3. "Lift your left foot, shake your foot, and count: one, two, three, four, five, six."
4. "Lift your right foot, shake your foot, and count: one, two, three, four, five."
5. "Raise your right arm, shake your hand, and count: one, two, three, four."

6. "Raise your left arm, shake your hand, and count: one, two, three."

7. "Lift your left foot, shake your foot, and count: one, two."

8. "Lift your right foot, shake your foot, and count to one."

9. "Thanks, everyone, and give yourselves a pat on the back. Everyone can be seated."

Mini Activity: Categories

Try this to . . . identify benefits or barriers to a challenge.

How It Works

- *Step 1*: The leader or guide articulates the challenge or problem a group is facing.
- *Step 2*: Someone is chosen as a caller. Someone else is chosen as a timekeeper.
- *Step 3*: All other players line up side by side, facing the caller and timekeeper.

- *Step 4*: The caller calls out a category that relates to the problem the guide or leader just articulated. For example, this could be being over budget, understaffed, etc.

- *Step 5*: The players then call out anything that relates to the challenge or problem. For example, if the category is budget, players may call out words like "small," "cutbacks," "more work," or "tired."

- *Step 6*: Then, the caller points at a player and says, "In 15 seconds or less, name a benefit or barrier to this challenge."

- *Step 7*: That player must identify either a benefit to solving the problem or a barrier to solving the problem. For example, a benefit could be reorganization, and a barrier could be low morale.

- *Step 8*: Players are eliminated from the game when they repeat an answer already given by another player or make up something that does not fit in the category.

- *Step 9*: The last player standing becomes the one who leads the post-engagement reflection. Reflection questions may be:
  - What can we glean from this experience?
  - What new insights did we gain?
  - How might we tweak this engagement to make it even more meaningful?

Mini Activity: Conveying the Alphabet

34

Try this to . . . build community.

How It Works

Everyone pairs up. There is a partner A and partner B. Partner A is the one with the shortest hair. Partner A begins a conversation with a sentence beginning with the letter "A." Partner B must continue the conversation with a sentence beginning with the letter "B." Partner A replies with a sentence beginning with the letter "C." The pair continues their conversation until they complete the alphabet.

For an extended experience, each pair starts a whole new conversation, working themselves backward through the alphabet. The conversation starts with the letter "Z" and ends when they reach the letter "A."

Mini Activity: Embrace The Change

Try this to . . . shift perspectives.

How It Works

- *Step 1*: Invite participants to stand in a relaxed position and then cross their arms. When all arms are crossed, ask everyone to uncross their arms and stand with their arms at their sides.

- *Step 2*: Ask, "Did anyone notice anything unusual? How did that feel?" Wait for various responses.

- *Step 3*: Then, ask everyone to cross their arms again, but this time, cross them the opposite way they normally cross their arms. People will have a bit of difficulty accomplishing this task, but give them time.

- *Step 4*: Once everyone has their arms crossed in the opposite way, ask everyone to stay in that position for a minute.

- *Step 5*: Ask, "Did you notice anything different? How did it feel after one minute? Did it begin to feel more natural?"

- *Step 6*: Lead a short reflection on lessons that can be drawn from simply changing the way one crosses their arms. Ask participants to consider organizational patterns or changes and how they might relate to the simple arm-crossing activity.

Mini Activity: Freeze Tag

Try this to . . . build spontaneity through storytelling.

How It Works

Begin by asking two participants to be "performers." Then, have everyone except the performers stand in a line. When you say "go," the two performers improvise a scene (any scene) until someone shouts, "Freeze!" The one who yelled (aka the freezer) must run in, tag out one of the frozen performers, assume their position, and begin a completely different scene.

For an alternative version of this exercise, the player standing at the front of the line is turned around and becomes "blind" to the action. Any other player in line can call "freeze," and the front player turns around, tags out a player, and begins a new scene.

37

Try this to . . . increase awareness.

How It Works

Everyone stands in a circle. Players exchange places with other players through a series of operations. The operations are:

- *Step 1*: Player A points to someone else in the circle.
- *Step 2*: The player being pointed at (Player B) sees Player A pointing and responds by saying, "Go!"
- *Step 3*: Player A acknowledges the pointing and walks toward Player B to take their spot.
- *Step 4*: As Player A walks over, Player B points to another player and repeats steps one through three.

Mini Activity: Good for Us

Try this to . . . build community.

How It Works

Everyone is standing. Someone yells, "Whoever likes football, move across the room!" All football lovers rush to the other side of the room. Once everyone arrives, everyone who moved shouts, "Good for us!"

Then, someone yells, "Whoever likes chocolate, move to the left side of the room!" All chocolate lovers head to the left side of the room. Once everyone arrives, they shout, "Good for us!"

The process continues as different people shout out different items and places around the world. Each time everyone arrives at the designated spot, they yell, "Good for us!"

After about three or four minutes, time is called. A quick reflection follows. The guide might ask:

- "What did we all learn?"
- "Any surprises?"
- "What topic did you want to hear called that wasn't?"
- "Do you look at your team members in a new light? If so, why?"

Mini Activity: Grin or Cringe

Try this to . . . build imagination.

How It Works

The facilitator, who is also the timekeeper, establishes an invisible stage in the middle of the room. Then, they divide the group into two teams of grinners and cringers. Grinners are always laughing or smiling while cringers are always scowling and never laugh. The two teams stand shoulder to shoulder on each side of the invisible stage. The teams face each other with the invisible stage between them. Now, the fun can begin.

The facilitator rings the bell. One grinner and one cringer step onto the invisible platform facing each other.

The grinner has 15 seconds to greet the cringer in any way possible to make the cringer smile or laugh. When the bell rings, the facilitator determines if the cringer smiled or laughed. If so, the cringer joins the grinners' team. On the other hand, if the grinner fails to make the cringer smile or laugh, the grinner must join the cringers' side.

Continue until only one cringer is left standing as the winner. Then, if everyone wants to extend the game, switch cringers into grinners and do it again, or make the winning cringers into a team to see which one lasts longer.

Quick reflection questions are simply: What was going on in your mind as you waited for your turn? What did we learn, and how might it be applied to our work?

Try this to . . . increase spontaneity through storytelling.

How It Works

A player begins a solo improvisation scene that can last no longer than three minutes. This scene must reflect something common to the whole group. It could be a scenario at work, a project everyone is involved in, or something common in life. The solo player's goal is to try to get as many people engaged in this scene as possible without actually calling them to join. The scene must be so compelling to the group that different members understand and see where they can join in.

As soon as someone in the group sees where they can join in, they call, "Freeze." Then, they begin a two-person scene with the first player. A third player does the same. As more players enter, the scene becomes larger and larger. At three minutes, time is called, and the last player to enter must create a new improvisation and has three minutes to start a new scene that others will join. In three minutes, time is called. The group votes if they want a third scene. If they do, then the last person to enter the last scene must start the third scene. If the group votes no, the facilitator calls an end to the engagements and starts a quick reflection with questions such as:

- What did the scenes represent?
- What does this tell us about our team or workspaces?
- What insights can be gleaned from the scenes?
- How might they inform new thinking and behaviors?

Mini Activity: Name Game

Try this to . . . raise energy levels and focus.

How It Works

- *Step 1:* Players stand in a circle and are given a few seconds to choose a pose that represents their name or their job. For example, if your name is Mary, you might give a big smile. If you are a nurse, you might pantomime giving someone a shot. The goal is for the group to identify if a pose is representing a name or a job and then guess the name or job.

  - Once everyone has decided on a pose, everyone shares their pose. Once the group guesses what everyone's pose is and what it means, the second step of the engagement begins.

- *Step 2*: The person with the closest birthday begins. They strike the pose of the person on their right.

If they remembered the pose correctly, then the person to the right does the same and strikes the pose of the person on *their* right. If they are correct, the process continues. Around the circle it goes.

- The goal is to get around the circle with no mistakes in two minutes or less. When someone makes a mistake, the group must begin at the start with the person with the closest birthday. Every team member is allowed two mistakes. At two mistakes, that player must drop out of the circle. The process continues without them; however, they are not out of the game. Their job is now to run around behind the circle, encouraging others with hints.

- *Step 3*: Once the group makes it all the way around the circle, the engagement ends. Players then engage in a quick reflection with questions such as:

  - How did it feel to strike a pose?
  - How did it feel to make a mistake?
  - How was it to be reminded or helped if you forgot a pose?
  - How did it feel when those at the beginning of step two got out when others were helped so they never got out?

Mini Activity: Oracle

Try this to . . . improve listening skills, raise energy, and encourage imagination.

How It Works

The first step is to create the Oracle, a group of four people who all sit in a row, one behind the other. The first person sits on the floor. The second person sits on a chair. The third person stands behind the person sitting on a chair. The fourth person stands on a chair behind the third person. That way, everyone can see all the faces of the Oracle.

Someone, other than the four people making up the Oracle, volunteers to be the host. The host then asks the rest of the participants for a big existential question. For example: what's the purpose of life? Where will I go after I die? Will Charles make a good king?

Once the host has a question, they then turn to the Oracle and repeat the question. The Oracle attempts to answer the question one word at a time (per person). When the Oracle is in action, everyone's arms wave to the side. When the Oracle is in silent contemplation, everyone's hands come together in a kind of "prayer" pose.

It's a daft yet funny engagement, and since the answer comes one word at a time, the Oracle can sound brilliant or just downright ridiculous!

Here's an example:

Audience question: What is love?

Oracle 1: Love

Oracle 2: is

Oracle 3: a

Oracle 4: warm

Oracle 1: latte

Oracle 2: in

Oracle 3: the

Oracle 4: morning

The game ends when the Oracle says, "No more questions."

Try this to . . . ignite happiness through a good gut workout.

How It Works

This is a very simple engagement, but for it to work, everyone must commit. It starts with someone volunteering to laugh. They keep laughing until someone else joins in. The goal is to get everyone in the group laughing. Anyone can laugh in any way they want, but they must keep laughing until everyone is doubled over in laughter.

Try this to … strengthen collaboration through storytelling.

Resources Required

- Story Master
- Storyteller
- Favorite Word Monitor
- Story Characters

How It Works

All players in the group are asked to write the following on slips of paper:

- A setting

- ○ Examples: in the forest, on the beach, inside a cave, etc.
- Two to four characters, though the group can add more people if desired. Each character has at least one distinguishing attribute.
  - ○ Examples: A grandmother with red hair who loves to go bowling, a young child who loves math but can't spell, a pirate that hates water, etc.
- A challenge or opportunity
  - ○ Examples: Heavy rain causes flooding, someone wins $1 million, a teenager works at their first job, etc.
- A time period
  - ○ Examples: Present day, the Roaring Twenties, the Middle Ages, etc.
- A color
  - ○ Examples: Red, blue, green, etc.
- An emotion
  - ○ Examples: Happy, sad, jealous, etc.
- A favorite word
  - ○ Examples: Sunshine, hippopotamus, canoodle, etc.

Once all players have filled in their suggestions on the slips of papers, the papers are placed in bowls according to their category: setting, character, challenge, time, color, emotion, and favorite word.

The story master takes one piece of paper from each of the bowls and shares it with the group so the framework of the story is known to everyone. Then, one player is chosen to be the storyteller. Other team members are chosen to be the characters in the story. One team member becomes the favorite word monitor. The favorite word monitor's job is to listen as the storyteller crafts the story and makes sure the favorite word is used at least 15 times.

Once everyone knows the story framework, those who are the characters in the story all lie on the floor. The storyteller then begins to tell the story. Every time a character is mentioned in the story, the person who represents the character pops up.

As soon as the storyteller uses all 15 favorite words, the favorite word monitor calls time, and the story comes to a quick end. Then, the group chooses if they like the way the story ended. If yes, the engagement ends. If the group votes no, they have 30 seconds to come up with a new ending before the storyteller calls time.

Try this to . . . raise energy levels and focus.

How It Works

Players stand in a circle. A player comes up with a unique sound and movement. The sound and movement are replicated from one person to the next until it reaches the originator. The originator then points to someone in the circle. That person instantly becomes the new originator and makes a new sound and movement for the group to replicate. The game ends when everyone has had a chance to be the originator.

Mini Activity: String of Pearls

Try this to . . . strengthen collaboration and storytelling skills.

How It Works

Players take turns telling a story one line at a time (the story is best delivered in the third person). Everyone stands side by side and imagines that the space in front of them represents the narrative timeline of the story being crafted. A player may step forward on any part of the timeline and present a story element. As more story elements are added to the timeline, the story emerges. Players must keep the logical build of the story going until it reaches a satisfactory end.

Mini Activity: The Blob

Try this to . . . raise energy and fun levels through movement and laughter.

How It Works

Everyone stands in an empty room. Each person has a folded paper in their hand, but only one person's paper has an "X" on it. At the sound of the bell, everyone opens their paper. The person with the "X" immediately begins to "tag" the others in the room. Once someone gets tagged, they join hands and stay connected. The members of the growing group continue running and tagging people while the shrinking members of the untagged group try to not get tagged. Everyone runs around the room while the connected group—The Blob—grows larger by the minute as more and more people get tagged. The Blob keeps going until it overtakes everyone in the room.

Try this to . . . create a sense of accomplishment.

How It Works

Players partner off and stand together. One of the pairs suggests an image, and their partner gives a title or a caption for that image. It can read like an inspirational quote, title, meme, or even hashtag. The pair tries to create five different memes in 60 seconds. Once the pair has completed five sets, they switch roles, and they have another 60 seconds to complete five more sets. Once each pair completes two complete sets of five, they yell, "Done!" The first pair done wins.

Mini Activities: The Wad

Try this to . . . raise energy and create laughter.

How It Works

Divide everyone into groups of three, four, or five, depending on the size of the team. Give each smaller group a large piece of construction paper or butcher paper, which the group quickly bunches up into a ball. The goal is to bat the paper wad around the group as many times as possible without letting it hit the floor; each team member must touch The Wad at least five times. The first group that reaches 35 bats without dropping it is the winner.

Try this to . . . raise energy and evoke laughter while supporting team members.

How It Works

Two players face off in a game of rock, paper, scissors—but instead, it's Tiger, Salesperson, Alien.

- Tiger: forms their hands into the shape of claws and roars, "GRRRRRR!"

- Salesperson: shakes hands and says, "Hi Ya."

- Alien: makes two antennas with their index fingers, which they hold at each side of their head while saying, "Take me to your leader."

Just as in rock, paper, scissors, there are winners and losers. In this case, the tiger beats the salesperson, the alien beats the tiger, and the salesperson beats the alien.

Once everyone is paired up, the leader counts, "One, two, three, shoot!" The players make a physical choice. The leader calls for the winners. All winners then pair up with other winners. The losers begin to cheer for the winner to whom they lost. Each round, the leader calls for the winners. The remaining winners pair up for another round. The losers keep cheering for those to whom they lost. The final round comes when only two winners remain. The final playoff has those who lost standing and cheering behind the last remaining winner of their group.

The final winner is cheered for by everyone. This is a fun, fast-moving, and *loud* activity.

Mini Activity: Triangle

Try this to . . . build energy and focus.

How It Works

All players mill about the room; they may not communicate with each other. The caller tells everyone to stop moving. Each player silently chooses two other players among the group to be their partners in forming an equilateral triangle. Once everyone says they have their chosen parents, the caller calls, "Go!" All the players must rush around the room finding their partners. Once people have found their partners, they stand in an equilateral triangle. The game ends when everyone finds their triangle.

101 Activities to Ignite Collaboration, Boost Creativity, and Fuel Innovation

Mini Activity: Yes, Let's

Try this to . . . build spontaneity, collaboration, and commitment.

How It Works

Players spread out across the room. A single player then suggests an activity to be performed, such as: "Everyone touch your toes!" Everyone shouts enthusiastically, "Yes, let's!" Then, they perform that activity. Everyone engages in that activity until another player suggests the next one with everyone saying, "Yes, let's!"

Try this to . . . build team spirit.

How It Works

Players stand in a circle. The team must count to 20; however, no one can speak except to call out a number. Numbers must be called out in consecutive order. Any team member can call the next number; however, no two team members may speak at the same time. If two players call out a number at the same time, everyone yells, "Yikes!" The group then must return to the number one and start the counting again. The game ends when the players successfully reach 20.

Mini Activity: Watch the Broom

Try this to . . . create movement while evoking fun and laughter.

How It Works

Now for something completely different! Everyone stands sideways in a circle holding a mop upright with their right hand. When the designated caller yells, "Go!" everyone must let go of their mop and step forward, trying to catch the mop or broom the teammate next to them was holding. The designated caller continues to yell, "Go!" as everyone rushes forward, trying to catch the mop or broom of the person next to them. If someone doesn't catch the mop or broom before it hits the floor, both the player and the mop or broom are out of the game. The game continues until there is only one player left. The caller can call, "Go!" as quickly, slowly, or randomly as they choose.

SECTION FIVE:
TOOLS for LEADING Change

Purpose:
Bringing out the best in people.

Are you ready to take your innovation skills to the next level? Well, listen up because I've got some inspiring news for you!

Innovation and the creative process are like a wild roller coaster ride—full of ups, downs, and unexpected twists and turns. It can feel chaotic and messy at times, but that's where the magic happens. And guess what? We've got just the thing to help you manage this beautiful mess: a whole range of innovative tools and processes!

So, take a deep breath and get ready to dive in because this section is packed with exciting resources to help you become a true innovation guide. You'll learn how to navigate the chaos and bring order to the madness. Trust us, with these tools and processes in your toolbox, there's no limit to what you can create. Let's get started on this adventure together!

Try this to . . . wrap up meetings in a meaningful way.

Meetings often don't allow enough time or space for everyone to weigh in, leaving participants feeling like they didn't get a chance to hear from everyone. The Ah-Ha Sign-Off can be a big help.

Benefits

- Gives everyone, even the quietest members of your team, a chance to weigh in

Resources Required

- Facilitator
- Team members attending a meeting

How It Works

At the close of an in-person or a virtual session, the facilitator calls for each participant to share their "ah-ha" takeaway from the meeting by typing it into the chat function. Each group member takes a few minutes to type what they want to share, and the facilitator reads each comment.

Typical Scenario

Zoë facilitated an incredibly productive virtual session that introduced a lot of new information. She feared that some important insights might go unheard. So, instead of ending the meeting, Zoë ended the discussion a few minutes early and invited everyone to share their insights or thoughts from the meeting in the chat. She read each text as it came through. Later, the participants said they felt encouraged and inspired by hearing what their team members had shared.

Beefing Up the Challenge

56

Try this to . . . better understand the larger context of a project or opportunity.

When facing a challenge you and your team are attempting to solve, you might not see the bigger picture, which can result in creating solutions that miss the mark. Beefing Up the Challenge can help broaden thinking and encourage better thinking.

Benefits

- Creates larger context for projects and illustrates both positive and negative aspects of a project or problem

Resources Required

- Beefing Up the Challenge form

How It Works

Before solving a problem, the team takes a few minutes to create context for a problem by considering both the positive potential and negative aspects of a solution or problem. Team members take two to three minutes to complete Beefing Up the Challenge form individually. Once everyone has completed the form, members share their responses, feedback, and ideas.

Typical Scenario

Julie felt her team was not seeing the bigger context of the problem they were being asked to solve. So, she asked her team to complete the Beefing Up the Challenge form and bring it to the department meeting. Everyone looked over the tool and said they were eager to respond.

Julie was concerned that the next meeting would dissolve into a big complaining fest. However, she was pleasantly surprised that the Beefing Up the Challenge form helped people better articulate their thoughts and see the challenge in its larger context.

Check-In, Check-Out

Try this to . . . start meetings with deeper intent and commitment.

Meetings, meetings, and more meetings. Sometimes, it's just too much. Energy, motivation, and interest suffers as one meeting morphs into another. It's hard to keep a team of people engaged. Participants need a way to be present and know they can leave when the event ends. Sounds obvious, right? It isn't. It's hard for people to rush from one meeting to another with any sense of presence. Check-In, Check-Out can help.

Benefits

- Increases chances for team members to be present and engaged

Resources Required

- Team members attending a meeting

How It Works

Check-In, Check-Outs are great bookends for any meeting to increase authenticity and commitment.

- *Checking In*: At the beginning of a meeting, the leader invites members to "check in" to the space. This can be as quick as, "I'm Karen, and I'm checking in." Or it could be a more elaborate activity. The check-in doesn't mean that every participant agrees with everything that's about to happen, but rather they commit to being present and attentive.

- *Checking Out*: The check-out gives finality and freedom to the meeting. It raises everyone's energy and adds a bit of fun to the meeting's conclusion. Checking out can be as easy as, "I'm Karen, and I'm checking out." Or the leader might ask everyone to check out with one word that sums up how they felt about the meeting: "I'm Karen, I feel encouraged, and I'm checking out." Finally, a check-out provides a sense of completion as members leave the meeting.

Typical Scenario

Dan started a meeting by inviting everyone to check in by stating their name. He gave an example: "Hi, I'm Dan, and I'm checking in." Dan then invited the group to follow suit. "Anyone can start," Dan said. One by one, all team members checked in.

At the close of the meeting, Dan invited everyone to check out. Again, he demonstrated: "I'm Dan, and I'm checking out." Everyone followed his lead. As each person checked out, the team nodded. When everyone had finished, participants got up to leave.

Additional Examples of Check-In, Check-Out

1. *Full Group Check-In, Check-Out:* Use this when time is short. The facilitator invites the whole team to check in or check out at the same time. The facilitator explains, "On the count of three, say your name and say, 'Checking in' (or 'Checking out,' depending on the situation)."

2. *That Reminds Me of Checking In:* When the group doesn't know each other and you have a bit more time, use this check-in. One person begins by saying their name and something interesting. For example, "I'm Jen, and I love horses."

   If that reminds someone else in the group of something, they would say, "I'm Jim, and that reminds me of the time my neighbor's horse got loose one New Year's night."

   If that reminds someone else in the group of something, they would say, "I'm Dan, and that reminds me of the New Year's party I attended where the host's house caught on fire." This continues as different members of the group are reminded of different things as more people check in. It's a fun and often funny way to get a group relaxed and acquainted.

3. *One Word or One Sentence Check-Ins:* These are simple check-ins that go quickly yet are engaging. Use the following to spark other ideas for rapid check-ins:

   a. Check in with one word that summarizes what you hope to accomplish during the meeting.

   b. Check in with one statement of what happened since our last meeting.

   c. Check in with how you are feeling.

   d. Check in with something new in your department.

4. *One Word or One Sentence Check-Outs:* These simple check-outs are powerful tools in that they let the group feel a sense of accomplishment and end the session. Many times, people leave a meeting or session feeling like nothing happened or changed. As with the check-ins, use the ideas below to generate other quick check-outs you can try with your team:

   a. Check out with one thing you got from the session or meeting.

   b. Check out with one word that describes how you feel.

   c. Check out with one sentence that explains what you will do before the next session or meeting.

   d. Check out with how this session or meeting changed or shifted in your thinking.

101 Activities to Ignite Collaboration, Boost Creativity, and Fuel Innovation

Critical Debate

Try this to . . . strengthen an idea or test its validity.

We get attached to our ideas so much that it's easy to fall in love with them. The problem? Our first ideas are rarely our best ones; rather, they are merely starting points, little bursts of inspiration that should serve as blueprints for further innovating. The best ideas are slowly cultivated and built upon. The Critical Debate tool helps a team work out the kinks of an idea and see how they might make the idea even better.

CRITICAL DEBATE

YOUR FIRST IDEA IS NOT YOUR BEST ONE, YET!
STRENGTHEN ANY IDEA WITH THIS SIMPLE PROCESS SHOWN BELOW:

IDEA: _____

WHAT IS GOOD ABOUT IT?   WHAT IS NOT GOOD?   TEAM A -HOW COULD IT WORK?

Benefits

- Clarifies the strengths and weaknesses of an idea to improve it

Resources Required

- Group to critically debate an idea

How It Works

Group members challenge an idea that came out of a brainstorming session and that they feel can be improved. Using the Critical Debate tool, members question what they see as good and bad about the idea. Team members offer constructive suggestions for tweaking ideas into something better. Then, it's up to the team to decide if the idea will withstand the critical debate and live to see another day.

Typical Scenario

Andrea had just presented an idea to her team. She knew the idea had merit but wasn't convinced how much. So, she invited her team to run a critical debate.

"Tell me what is wrong with my idea," she said, "and then tell me how to fix it." At first, no one wanted to criticize her idea, but one brave member spoke up.

"I like the idea," he said, "but I don't think it goes far enough."

"How can I take it further?" Andrea asked.

Someone else from the group chimed in, encouraging other team members to speak up. After that, the team was on a roll, and the critiques continued taking Andrea's original concept to a new level. The team no longer worried if they were hurting anyone's feelings and instead fell into the groove of building up an idea. The team kept tweaking the idea a good 30 minutes before they felt the idea had merit.

In the end, everyone could see how taking the time for a Critical Debate illuminated how their original idea was weak. They never would have understood this or how to improve upon it without the rigorous discussion the Critical Debate fosters.

Dang-Sure Hat

Try this to . . . ensure a team does its best work.

Teams often suggest solutions before they understand the problem. They chomp at the bit to start creating solutions before anyone has had the chance to do a deep dive and learn about the challenge, problem, or opportunity. The Dang-Sure Hat is a reminder for teams to make sure they understand the real problem before they start solving the problem.

Benefits

- Keep a team on their best game

Resources Required

- Hat
- Dang-Sure monitor

How It Works

Whenever a solution or big idea is presented, it's a great time to put on the Dang-Sure Hat to ensure the best possible outcome. At the beginning of the project, a team member volunteers to serve as the Dang-Sure monitor. Members can take turns serving in this crucial role. Any kind of hat works for the Dang-Sure Hat. We used an Indiana-Jones-type hat because we thought it was cool, but any hat will do.

The Dang-Sure monitor's job is to ensure the team does their best possible work and not let the following happen: rushing into a solution before gathering enough information, overlooking a group member, being married to certain ideas, more assertive members hijacking the group, or forgetting vital information. The Dang-Sure monitor stops the team when they feel the group is misstepping. The Dang-Sure monitor allows the group to move forward *only* when the group feels they have adequately addressed the Dang-Sure monitor's concern.

Typical Scenario

Lucy's supervisor asked her and her team to solve a significant challenge. Lucy's team had already gathered some information about the problem. As a result, many team members believed they knew what to do, so they began pushing hard to create a solution. Lucy was concerned that the team really wasn't ready to decide on a solution and needed more information. So, she brought out the Dang-Sure Hat and introduced it to her team. Then, she assigned a team member, Doug, to be the Dang-Sure Hat monitor. Doug would make sure the team did not rush to a solution before everyone really understood the problem.

Lucy explained, "Doug, the monitor, will remain in place for the duration of the project. Doug will help the team get the best possible solution by asking questions that need an answer."

With that, Lucy urged her team to carry on with the help of Doug. It wasn't long before someone suggested a solution. That was the signal for the Dang-Sure Hat monitor to step in with questions like:

- "Is this solution based on actual needs that have been identified?"
- "Have you heard from your customers/clients as to what they actually need?"
- "Have you taken the time to consider the larger context of this solution?"
- "What other ideas does the team have that are not being heard?"
- "Who else needs to weigh in before you decide on a solution?"
- "What might you be missing?"

The monitor's job was simple: hold the team accountable to create the best possible solution, not just the easy one or the one they might want.

In Lucy's case, the Dang Sure Hat monitor was a huge help. She was confident that they needed to learn more before designing a practical solution; however, she was not able to get her team to slow down and consider other options or check to see if the solution was really relevant. Fortunately, Lucy did not need to fight this battle alone, thanks to the Dang-Sure Hat monitor who kept questioning the group.

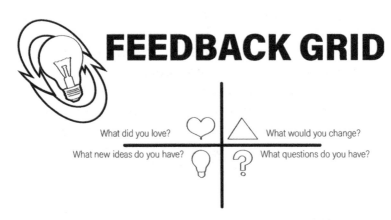

FEEDBACK GRID

What did you love? | What would you change?

What new ideas do you have? | What questions do you have?

Try this to . . . create an effective way to give and receive feedback.

Feedback is a gift. There is no such thing as bad feedback; it's all just information. The Feedback Grid improves the quality of both giving and receiving feedback.

Benefits

- Provides space for effective feedback

Resources Required

- Feedback Grid
- Pencil or pen

How It Works

When a person needs feedback, the Feedback Grid is very helpful. Often, people don't know how to give feedback, so the grid proves a helpful guide. The person seeking feedback invites individuals to provide feedback and explains the Feedback Grid. That person then presents his ideas or project. At that point, those providing feedback capture their feedback on the Feedback Grid. Once the feedback session is over, the person requesting the feedback gathers the Feedback Grids to analyze the feedback and incorporate it. The Feedback Grids improves the quality of feedback by providing options for feedback.

The Feedback Grid has four quadrants, but not all the quadrants need to be completed, only those that apply to the person giving feedback:

- What do you like?
- What would you change?
- What questions emerged?
- What new ideas bubbled up?

Garden Gander

Try this to . . . prepare a team for stellar brainstorming.

A common reason for ineffective brainstorming is failing to properly prepare. This can result in underdeveloped concepts, surface-level ideas, or settling for any random idea. Garden Gander provides a way for people to prepare for brainstorming, thus avoiding common pitfalls.

Benefits

- Generates new ideas

Resources Required

- An inspiring place to brainstorm

How It Works

Before a brainstorming session, each member takes a few minutes to reflect on the problem. The goal is to come up with at least one idea to bring to the brainstorm session. This happens in an inspiring place, i.e sitting under a tree, in the courtyard, on a bench in a nearby park, or even just going for a walk.

Typical Scenario

Matthew's team was about to begin to brainstorm. Matthew knew that, if everyone had a few minutes to reflect on the challenge, they would likely come up with better ideas. So, Matthew asked everyone to find a quiet spot in a nearby park and reflect on the project. Team members enjoyed this break. Many commented that the break freed up mental space, giving them a better perspective on the challenge and making it easier for ideas to bubble up.

Ice, Water, Steam

Try this to . . . capture data in a holistic, nontraditional way.

Collecting data on projects or services isn't always easy. Sometimes, it's clear what we can measure; other times, it's not. We need ways to collect data that takes into consideration the complexity of today's world. Ice, Water, Steam is a start.

Benefits

- Presents a way for holistic data gathering and reporting

How It Works

With this tool, projects are labeled either "ice," "water," or "steam."

- Ice refers to projects that have easy-to-quantify, *hard* outcomes, such as improved patient scores, reduced number of complaints, or lower costs.
  - Example: People enrolled in a pre-diabetic program all develop successful physical activity and nutritional habits, resulting in significant improvements to their blood work.
- Water refers to projects that have specific results but continue to morph.
  - Example: A local animal shelter becomes overrun with dogs and cats. However, no one seems to want to adopt pets. So, the team decides to make a social media account for the dogs and cats ready to be adopted. Over time, these accounts increase adoptions and raise awareness of volunteer opportunities at the shelter. This leads to increased funding because one of the volunteers is a grant writer. The shelter can then help more animals, which makes it possible to hire more paid staff. This leads to creating a pet foster program, which enables the shelter to add simple pet care classes to their services.

- Steam refers to projects in which things get better, but it's unclear precisely why.
    - Subtle transformations are hard to quantify. Data can capture *what* happened but doesn't always tell us *why* something happened. I think it's because these are matters of the heart.
    - Example: An international group works to improve communications between their US and global offices. As they work on the project, simple adjustments are made but nothing major, yet everything seems to improve. When the team tries to pinpoint what improved and why, they can't precisely tell what made the difference. So, in the end, the leader said, "Sometimes, we don't need to know why things get better but celebrate the fact that they did."

Game Changers

BTDTBCDB

No Brainers

Parking Lot

Try this to . . . sort multiple ideas to choose ones with the highest potential.

Teams often come up with so many ideas that team members become overwhelmed. Idea Sort helps teams sort their ideas, identify those with the most potential, and move forward.

Benefits

- Helps to sort ideas

Resources Required

- Idea grid, whiteboard, or poster

How It Works

Generating ideas is just the first step. Choosing the one with the highest potential is the critical next step, but with lots of ideas, it can be hard to choose. The group starts by sorting the ideas into four different categories:

- Game changers
- BTDTBCDB (Been There Done That, But Could Do Better)
- No brainers
- Parking

Once sorting is completed, the group can vote on which idea(s) to move forward.

Typical Scenario

After brainstorming, Koen's team had so many ideas that they didn't know what to do next. A facilitator suggested the Idea Sort grid. Koen went first and placed an idea, captured on a Post-it Note, in the categories they felt best suited it. Team members followed. Everyone was invited to agree or disagree on where ideas should go. Even the quieter members spoke up.

Once ideas were sorted into categories, the team voted on which ideas they wanted to pursue. Sorting ideas helps teams manage multiple ideas, simplify the problem, and put them on a better path to finding a solution that might have otherwise eluded them.

Imagimeet

Try this to . . . foster healthy conversation between bosses and direct reports.

Sometimes a team member needs to talk to a boss outside of normal meeting times. But how can such a meeting happen when no provision exists for it? Imagimeet fills this gap.

Benefits

- Normalizes need for transparent employee-employer conversations

Resources Required

- Boss willing to hold Imagimeets
- Team members willing to schedule them

How It Works

An Imagimeet is an informal conversation between a boss and employee that the employee calls. The purpose of the Imagimeet is when an employee needs to talk to their boss. The ground rules of the Imagimeet are:

- Once an employee requests an Imagimeet, it must happen within 48 hours.

- Imagimeets are held outside of the office. Common places are the company cafe, lobby, garden, or local coffee shop—pretty much anywhere except the boss's office. When it happens off campus, it may help to ask a third person to join.

- Imagimeets last between 15 and 45 minutes or, rarely, even an hour.

- Imagimeets don't have a rigid structure; they're simply a time for a conversation.

- If the Imagimeet takes place in a space like a coffee shop, the boss buys the coffee.

Typical Scenario

Jordan struggled to connect and collaborate with a co-worker and needed some advice. While Jordan didn't want to throw the co-worker under the bus, they needed help to navigate the relationship and believed their boss might have some ideas. So, they requested an Imagimeet.

Jordan and the boss met in a garden opposite of the office building. The boss gave Jordan some good advice, and both returned to work feeling better. Jordan considered the problem solved, and the boss felt better informed.

Try this to . . . keep team members engaged.

Ever feel like you'd benefit from a mental break to jump start your creativity? Most companies aren't set up to pay employees to take regular afternoons off. The best you will get is the regular vacation days. Inspired Afternoons are not "vacation days," but opportunities to get out to explore, learn, gain new perspectives, and get re-energized.

Benefits

- Increases team engagement and motivation

Resources Required

- Willing spirit
- Sense of adventure
- Few hours

How It Works

When your teams need an energy boost or a reset, give them an Inspiring Afternoon. It could be an hour, three hours, or the whole afternoon. Most of the time, it's a segment of a day, and you can keep it really low-key. All your team needs is a little change of pace and some new scenery. While on this mini adventure, your team will hopefully be refreshed and discover new insight. When you return from your Inspired Afternoon, ask team members to share their discoveries with the whole team.

It's simple and doesn't cost a thing, just a little time. You or your team member choose an afternoon to go experience something new like the library, a local park, a new business, people watching, a neighboring city, an old town, or a construction site. The place doesn't need to be unique; some could revisit somewhere like it's the first time. The goal is to expand one's thinking. Get out of the doldrums, and see what's happening.

Typical scenario

After three weeks of working 60 hours, Lisa was tired. She needed a quick lift. Fortunately, her boss supported the idea of Inspired Afternoons. So, Lisa took off and drove 12 miles to a neighboring lakeside city. She simply sat on the dock and watched. Fishing boats came and went. An artist dropped by and started painting. Three older men, laughing loudly, made their way to the lakeside and set their remote-control sailboats adrift. She watched as the three sailboats floated around the lake.

She spoke to the people who happened by the dock. The artist was trying to paint every lake in Florida. She learned why the fishing crew only fished on Wednesdays.

She was moved by the three men, widowers, who met every Wednesday afternoon to sail their boats and grab an early dinner afterward. It was the highlight of their week.

After several hours, Lisa gathered up her chair, returned to her team, and inspired by all she saw, couldn't wait to share. Each time someone returned from an Inspired Afternoon and shared their new learnings with the team, everyone became energized, expanded their horizons, and got new ideas, and best of all, it didn't cost a penny.

Lifeguard Facilitation (LGF)

Try this to . . . lead with a light touch.

Lifeguard Facilitation, LGF, is a guide for a group. Its purpose is to keep a space safe, see that every member feels visible and heard, and authentically move the group forward while also keeping all the work on the team's shoulders.

Benefits

- Aids in facilitating with a light touch

Resources Required

- Person willing to be a Lifeguard Facilitator

How It Works

Think of real lifeguards sitting on the sidelines at a local swimming pool and keeping swimmers safe. They blow a whistle if someone runs, dunks another swimmer, or starts causing a ruckus. If someone needs a lifeline, they toss them one. Lifeguards make sure everyone knows the rules. In short, they keep the pool safe and hold swimmers accountable.

Lifeguard Facilitators (LGFs) do the same thing, except they aren't in the water and the group isn't swimming. At the core of being an LGF is the "humility pledge." The humility pledge refers to the process of acknowledging that the group they're leading has lots of wisdom and probably already knows the answers. The LGF's goal is simply to keep the space safe so the group can do their important work and get to where they need to go.

The roles and tasks of the LGF are as follows:

- Remains humble and always respects the group.
- Invites everyone to check in at the beginning of the session and check out at the close (Engagement #57).
- States the purpose of meeting and clarify its goals.
- Establishes session expectations and roles, such as a scribe or Dang-Sure monitor, (Engagement #59).
- Reminds participants that everyone has permission and a responsibility to participate.
- Leads dialogue without saving the group, but rather gives the gift of struggling through the problem-solving process.
- Invites the group to reflect on goals or new learnings at appropriate times.

- Does not let quiet members hide behind more talkative ones; invites everyone to talk.

- Assigns a Dang-Sure monitor who ensures everyone shares, stays involved, and calls out hijackers.

- Reminds the group there are two kinds of group hijackers: quiet and loud. Both are damaging to a group.

- Keeps the group focused. With the more rigid members of the group, creative work follows a non-linear pathway.

- Ends each session with a next step that identifies who will do what and by when.

Make Your Mark

Try this to . . . make your notetaking or scribing come alive and be memorable.

Everyone can zip up their notetaking or scribing with a few simple sketches. Yes, anyone! Make Your Mark uses simple drawings to help spruce up presentations, create snappy notes, and give scribing a lift.

Benefits

- Brings your notetaking alive, engages people, and makes you look more fun and creative

Resources Required

- Writing utensil
- Whiteboard, SMART Board, or paper of some kind

How It Works

If you can draw a straight line or a circle (that's almost everyone), you can pretty much draw anything. We're not talking about Rembrandt here, but rather simple ways to make your scribing and notetaking surprising and delightful. Check out the graphic below. Next time you are asked to take notes or scribe, put some of the ideas below to good use.

101 Activities to Ignite Collaboration, Boost Creativity, and Fuel Innovation

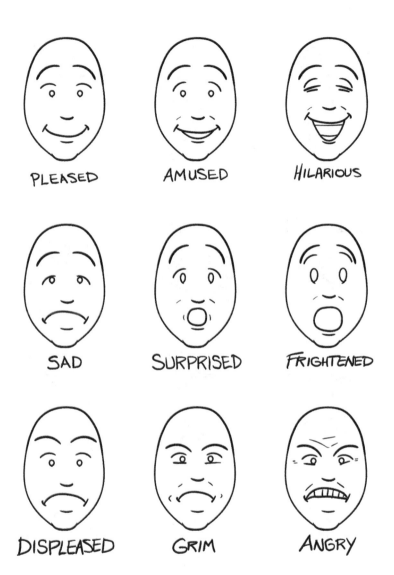

PLEASED   AMUSED   HILARIOUS

SAD   SURPRISED   FRIGHTENED

DISPLEASED   GRIM   ANGRY

101 Activities to Ignite Collaboration, Boost Creativity, and Fuel Innovation

Typical Scenario

Janelle and her team had a big challenge ahead of them: presenting the outcomes of their recent project to some weary big bosses at the end of a long day. But Janelle knew that a typical PowerPoint or bland handout just wouldn't cut it. So, she came up with a creative idea: instead of boring slides, each team member would use simple line drawings to illustrate their portion of the report.

At first, Janelle's team was nervous about this approach. But as each person stepped up to the SMART Board and shared their sketch, the bosses were captivated. By the end of the presentation, it was clear that Janelle's team had knocked it out of the park.

Not only did they succeed in capturing the bosses' interest, but one of the bosses was so impressed that they asked Janelle to prepare a similar presentation for the next town hall meeting. Janelle was overjoyed by the recognition and the success of her team's innovative approach.

Meet Grinders

Try this to . . . create super short meetings with a top leader.

Top leaders are pressed for time. Finding time to meet with them in a timely fashion can be almost impossible. Meet Grinders provides a healthy way to communicate outside the hierarchy when necessary.

Benefits

- Improves agile communication across the organization

Resources Required

- Stopwatch

How It Works

A Meet Grinder is a rapid, concise meeting designed to keep information flowing and a project moving. When a team is stuck or needs information quickly, there often isn't time to wait for a scheduled meeting with a leader, which could take three or four weeks. Instead, a team requests a Meet Grinder. The Meet Grinder never lasts more than five minutes, and all members stand up during the meeting.

Typical Scenario

Molly needed to confirm that a particular project would interest her organization. She asked for a Meet Grinder with two leaders. Since the Meet Grinder had become an accepted part of the organization's innovation ecosystem, Molly sent off a text asking for a meeting, confident she would hear back from them as soon as possible. Sure enough, Molly found herself in front of the leader within an hour. In a few well-crafted sentences, she presented her request. The leaders gave their input, Molly thanked them, and both parties went on their way.

Merry Metaphor Maker

Try this to . . . create a way to clarify a point or thought.

When a team or group is trying to solve a problem or clarify an idea, creating a metaphor often broadens thinking and deepens understanding, so people can imagine a new way to see what they are working on. Creating metaphors and then sharing with the group is a powerful and memorable way to strengthen an idea or make a good solution even better.

101 Activities to Ignite Collaboration, Boost Creativity, and Fuel Innovation

Benefits

- Makes a complex idea understandable and memorable

How It Works

To create a metaphor:

1. Choose a character, object, or setting.

2. Focus on a particular scene you're describing.

3. Think of some other objects that share characteristics you mentioned in Step 1.

4. Name your metaphor and expand on it.

Story Arc

Try this to ... share a project outcome in a very short yet powerful way.

Time and time again, I see teams or individuals give presentations, only to drive the audience to their phones. No one wants that. Story Arc is a simple, four-minute presentation that is sure to engage your audience if not because of its subject, then because of its length.

Benefits

- Provides a powerful way to share stories

Resources Required

- Story Arc template

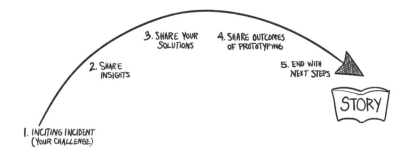

101 Activities to Ignite Collaboration, Boost Creativity, and Fuel Innovation

How It Works

Story Arc begins with activating an event that is the challenge or opportunity a team is encountering, followed by new insights or discoveries, ideas or solutions, feedback, and next steps.

- *Step 1*: The Why—the activating event, pressing problem, or compelling opportunity
- *Step 2*: New insights—what the team has learned about the situation
- *Step 3*: New ideas and solutions
- *Step 4*: Feedback received
- *Step 5*: Next steps

Section Six:

Problem-Solving in 60 minutes or less

Purpose:

Helping teams move, think differently, and collaborate.

Who says it takes forever to change the world? In situations where time is limited and deadlines are looming, these 60-minute (or less) engagements can be just what you need. The models presented in this section were born out of necessity when my team and I were tasked with facilitating rapid-cycle problem-solving for other teams. Designed to produce quick results, the models in this section are meant to generate solutions or prototypes that can be refined and tested through iterations, helping teams get a move on. Overall, they offer a fun and friendly way to tackle pressing challenges.

Dynamic Discussion

Try this to . . . address a generalized nagging problem.

When there's a nagging problem that plagues several departments or teams and no one seems to be the owner or problem-solver, Dynamic Discussion comes in handy. It's a non-threatening, inclusive way to address a problem, untapped opportunity, or resource.

Benefits

- Facilitates rapid-cycle problem-solving

Resources Required

- Guide willing to initiate discussion

How It Works

The guide welcomes the group and defines and clarifies the problem. Each group member offers their perspective, and questions are asked to clarify the problem. When the group feels ready, it votes on the following options with each member getting two votes:

1. Can the problem be solved with the information that has been shared in this session?
2. Is more time needed to solve this challenge?
3. Do other people need to be involved to really solve the problem?

After the vote, next steps are created. The group decides who will do what by when. The guide then thanks everyone for coming and dismisses the group.

Typical Scenario

Michelle, the head nurse for several units, faced a nagging problem. She knew something had to be done, so when she learned about Dynamic Discussion, she spun into action. She called the group together and invited everyone to share their perspective on the problem. She encouraged questions. When she felt the group was ready, she led the vote for a solution. Once the votes were counted, the group identified next steps and handed out assignments. The group expressed appreciation for the Dynamic Discussion. Several expressed surprise that the solution was there all along; they just didn't take the time to problem-solve.

Feedforward

Try this to . . . illustrate that feedback is a gift.

Sometimes, you need a way to send your problems out to the universe to see what the world has to say. But how? Marshall Goldsmith has the answer: *Feedforward*.[2]

Benefits

- Develops skills in giving and receiving feedback

Resources Required

- Feedback template
- Pen or pencil

How It Works

- *Step 1*: Participants write down something they want to get better at—an aspiration. For example, someone may want to be a better listener, exercise regularly, or call mom more often.

- *Step 2*: Put 15 minutes on the clock, and direct participants to find a partner. Once in pairs, each person will share their aspiration. Then, their partner gives a corresponding piece of advice. As each participant receives feedback, all they say is, "Thank you."

- *Step 3*: After both partners have shared and received advice, they put their hand in the air, indicating they need a new partner. Others doing the same will connect with the new partner. Repeat Step 2 until each participant has talked to six people.

- *Step 4*: Once time is called, everyone returns to their seats and is given a few minutes to reflect on the advice they received. They write at least one thing they will do differently.

- *Step 5*: Group members are given the opportunity to share their learnings and next steps.

Hack-a-Thon

Try this to . . . rally a group for rapid problem-solving.

Hack-a-Thon is a rapid-cycle, empathic problem-solving approach that can jump start problem-solving for any team facing a large or small challenge or opportunity.

Benefits

- Provides a pathway for teams to address pressing problems

Resources Required

- Facilitator
- Place to work
- Team willing to work rapidly

How It Works

- *Step 1*: A leader approves the running of a Hack-a-Thon and chooses a facilitator as a host.

- *Step 2*: A date is set, and participants are invited to join and told the topic, problem or opportunity of the Hack-a-Thon.

- *Step 3*: Participants who accept the invitation are instructed to connect with at least two individuals experiencing the problem the Hack-a-Thon is addressing. For example, say a company wants to address employee absenteeism in order to better serve the customer. So, the Hack-a-Thon participant will seek out and gain empathy for the people in the company who are often absent or never absent and for bosses who deal with high levels of absenteeism or those who don't. The goal is to learn from these people by hearing their stories and capturing their emotions and, if possible, go to where they experience the problem and shadow or observe them there. This prework of discovery and deep dive empathy gathering provides the Hack-a-Thon participants with fresh, first-hand knowledge of the problem, so they will bring their new insights to the Hack-a-Thon.

- *Step 4*: The Hack-a-Thon officially begins with team members sharing the new learnings they gained from their observations. Once the team unpacks these discoveries, articulates the root of the problem, and identifies the needs, the team moves to a rapid-cycle idea generation session.

- *Step 5*: When the team feels they have enough good ideas, they vote on their favorite ones. Then, they quickly create tangible, low-resolution prototypes, which are rough examples of their best ideas. Each prototype is created to illustrate how their ideas work.

- *Step 6*: Finally, they devise a way to test these prototypes with end users. If time doesn't allow the team to test the prototype on the day of the Hack-a-Thon, the team creates a testing plan time and schedules follow-up meetings to share the test results and any additional feedback. All feedback gathered from the testing is then captured and shared at a later meeting. Likewise, all input from the testing is captured.

- *Step 7*: The Hack-a-Thon moves the group forward and gets them on the road to solving the problem.

74

Try this to . . . build a safety net for a risky idea or project.

Many projects never get off the ground simply because they are deemed risky. Yet, no one will know the risk if they don't at least try. The Jump Start Manifesto gives such projects a chance.

Benefits

- Provides an iterative process for potentially risky projects

Resources Required

- Charter template or form
- Leader's signature

How It Works

The Jump Start Manifesto is a declaration of a project's potential risk, vision, goals, and milestones that show how a project, deemed risky, can start in an iterative way to ensure safety. Each stage or milestone included in the Jump Start Manifesto requires approval. At any point, the project can be stopped.

The Jump Start Manifesto template allows a team to articulate the project's risks and how those risks will be addressed in each milestone. Once a team has completed the Jump Start Manifesto, it is then presented to the leader for approval.

The Jump Start Manifesto

Project Name: _____

Project Rationale: _____

Perceived Risks: _____

Scope: _____

Risk Factors Addressed: _____

Milestones: _____

Approving Leader: _____

Go-No-Go Sign-Off: _____

Team Members: _____

Typical Scenario

Jackie and her team wanted to run a project. Her leaders felt it was risky, yet Jackie knew the project would help the company. Jackie used the Jump Start Manifesto to frame the project in iterative milestones. That way, the risk factor could be monitored at each phase, and the project could be halted at any point. A timeline was created, and touch-point meetings were scheduled. The project was on a trial basis, but at least there was movement that allowed new information to emerge.

| *Frustrations* | *Perfect World* | *Next Steps* |

Try this to . . . help co-workers deal with an organizational mandate.

Management's mandates are often the cause of great frustration, yet the team must accept them and move forward regardless. Innovate Anything, Anywhere can help a team rally around a mandate.

Benefits

- Maintains employee and team engagement

Resources Required

- Whiteboard or poster board for writing
- Sharpies

How It Works

Innovate Anything, Anywhere is a 60-minute process designed to help teams deal with a mandate. It has three stages: 1) capturing team frustrations, 2) articulating the group's perfect work world, and 3) creating that perfect work world while managing the mandate.

- *Step 1*: The team spends 15 minutes capturing their frustrations about the mandate on a whiteboard or poster.

- *Step 2*: The team spends another 15 minutes capturing their ideas of a perfect work world on the whiteboard or poster.

- *Step 3*: The team spends 30 minutes generating ideas and prototyping. The team explores how their frustrations can be flipped into positives to help create their perfect work world while still honoring the mandate. Prototypes are quickly built that reflect how the team will move forward. After a quick conversation about the next steps, team members commit to giving their solutions a good college try.

Typical Scenario

Matais's team was upset by a new leadership mandate, so they decided on an Innovate Anything, Anywhere. The team captured all their mandate frustrations and then articulated their perfect world. Matais noticed the team's attitude shift as they created ways to use the mandate to improve their own work experience.

Try this to . . . identify a team's assumptions.

When teams are trying to solve a problem or think creatively, assumptions can wreak havoc. The Know and Assume (K&A) engagement helps teams surface their hidden assumptions.

Benefits

- Identifies hidden assumptions and fosters open-mindedness

Resources Required

- Post-its
- Sharpies
- K&A template

How It Works

Participants work in groups of four or five. Each group has a station with a whiteboard or posters that have the words "know," "assume," and "powerful questions" written in large letters.

- Know: What do we know about this project or situation?
- Assume: What do we assume about the project or situation?
- Powerful Questions: What questions about the project are unanswered?

Next, the team populates the columns with their "knowledge" and "assumptions" about the problem or opportunity they are facing. As the groups list their K&As, powerful questions begin to emerge and are captured.

After about 20 to 30 minutes, the group leader invites the group to begin a round-robin tour of the other groups' stations. Groups move clockwise around the room, spending three to five minutes at each station reading what the other groups wrote. Participants leave notes such as, "Is this true? Really? What about this? What about that?" Once all the groups have visited every station, they return to their original station and review the notes left for them by the other groups.

Typical Scenario

Janelle was concerned that hidden assumptions hindered her team's progress. So, she divided the team into small groups and, using the K&A form, asked each member to identify what they know and assumed about the problem they were attempting to solve. She also asked the team to capture all of the powerful questions that emerged. Janelle instructed the groups to think about the problem they were working on and fill in the three columns with their own reactions.

After 20 minutes, Janelle invited the teams to circulate around the room in round-robin style to see what the other groups wrote. She encouraged them to write out their reactions to the other teams and leave them either on the board or on Post-its. After the round robin, everyone returned to their original places to debrief on what they had seen.

After each group had ample time to discuss the round robin, Janelle asked the groups to identify their biggest assumption. Each group's assumption(s) were recorded and kept for future use. All boards were photographed. Janelle thanked everyone for their contributions.

Peer Prodder

Try this to . . . get peers' perspectives on an idea or thought.

There are times when you have an idea that isn't fully formed and need help to develop it to its full potential. This is not the time to go to your superior or boss. It's your peers' expertise that you need. Peer Prodder is used to help an individual think deeper and broader about a particular issue they are pondering. The idea is to tap into peers' wisdom to get new perspectives on a situation or event. Only peers are invited to participate.

Benefits

- Fosters peer support

Resources Required

- Peers willing to give an hour of their time
- Refreshments
- Writing materials

How It Works

The host initiating the Peer Prodder invites a small group of peers to come together and listen to a specific idea the host is pondering. The peers' role is to be a reflector that provides new perspectives, not solutions or answers.

- *Step 1*: The host presents the idea they are pondering.
- *Step 2*: Peers quietly listen, take notes, and ask clarifying questions.
- *Step 3*: Each peer finds a quiet corner and reflects on what the host shared. In the reflection process, the peer creates a metaphor that provides a new way for the host to consider or apply the situation.
- *Step 4*: The peers are called back together and share their metaphors with the host.
- *Step 5*: Once each peer has shared, the host asks any clarifying questions.
- *Step 6*: The host thanks the peers for their time and thoughtful consideration. They ask their peers for any of their notes that might be helpful in the future. The host also asks the peers to keep the information shared in the Peer Prodder confidential.

Typical Scenario

Kyle had an idea brewing. He didn't know if it was good, but the idea kept coming back. So, he invited a small group of peers to hear him out and provide new perspectives. On the scheduled day, the peers met in Kyle's office. Kyle welcomed everyone, thanked them for their time, and invited them to enjoy his prepared refreshments.

He then outlined the Peer Prodder process. He presented his idea while each peer listened quietly. Then, each member took about 10 minutes to reflect on what they just heard and create a metaphor that captured the situation. After about 30 minutes, the group gathered, and the peers took turns sharing their metaphors and perspectives on the host's situation. Kyle then asked clarifying questions.

Kyle thanked everyone for coming, collected his guests' feedback sheets and notes, and used them for further review and consideration.

Power Hour

Try this to . . . get lots of ideas from a new set of people.

Power Hour creates a way for a team or company to garner ideas from a wide range of people who are from different backgrounds but are all affected by the problem they are trying to solve.

Benefits

- Builds collaboration and buy-in through idea generation

Resources Required

- Bell
- Large poster board or whiteboard
- One index card for every participant
- Room or open space
- Pencils or pens

How It Works

The Power Hour is a diverse idea-generation session. Participants come from a wide range of backgrounds but are all affected by the same problem. The Power Hour proceeds as follows:

- *Step 1*: The guide welcomes the participants and introduces the topic and instructions.
- *Step 2*: The guide shares the problem statement with the team and displays it where all can see and refer to it during the Power Hour.
  - Example: How might more employees participate in the organization's new health program? How might we revolutionize our customer experience?
- *Step 3*: The guide then challenges the group with this question: "If you were the most courageous person in the world and didn't care what anyone

thought, what ideas or solutions would you offer up that would solve the problem we are facing?"

- *Step 4*: Each participant receives an index card and writes the numbers one through five on the back of the index card five times.

- *Step 5*: When the bell sounds, participants individually write on the front of the index card: 1) one idea or solution to the problem and 2) one bold first step.

- *Step 6*: When the bell rings again, participants stop writing and find someone with whom they can share their idea and first step. Each person shares. Then, each pair exchanges their index cards with each other and rates the idea on the card on a one-to-five scale. At this point, no one should have their original card and idea.

- *Step 7*: The bell rings again, and everyone finds a new partner. Repeat the process five times.

- *Step 8*: Once five rounds of sharing ideas and voting have been completed, time is called. Everyone individually adds the scores on the back of their card. If a card doesn't have five scores, average the score.

- *Step 9*: The guide calls for scores: "Who has ideas that have a score of 25?" Everyone holding a card with an idea score of 25 raises their hand. An assigned scribe quickly writes the ideas and first steps on the board for all to see. Ideas that are duplicated or very similar are combined.

- *Step 10*: Then, the facilitator asks the group, "Whose card has a score of 24?" People raise their hands.

A new scribe captures those ideas and bold first steps, combining similar or duplicated ideas.

- *Step 11*: The facilitator calls for scores of 23. The people with a score of 23 raise their hands, and a new scribe captures those ideas, combining similar or duplicated ideas.

- *Step 12*: At this point, the ideas (scores of 25, 24, and 23) and the bold first steps have been written on the board for all to see. The guide calls for clarifying questions.

- *Step 13*: Then, the facilitator invites the participants to vote for their favorite idea and first step. Participants vote by placing a check or sticker on the idea they chose. Everyone gets two votes.

- *Step 14*: Scores are tabulated, and the top idea is chosen. If two or more ideas tie, the facilitator calls for another vote on the top two favorite ideas, or the group can decide to move both ideas forward.

- *Step 15*: The facilitator calls for any additions to the idea's first steps. Once everyone has an opportunity to weigh in, the facilitator thanks everyone for joining the Power Hour, and the Power Hour ends.

101 Activities to Ignite Collaboration, Boost Creativity, and Fuel Innovation

Try this to... get expert feedback on a specific prototyped solution or idea.

Prototype Push creates a way to get relevant feedback from those who know best.

Benefits

- Provides a quick and easy way to get feedback from experts

Resources Required

- Subject matter experts
- Prototype

How It Works

The Prototype Push is a feedback session where subject matter experts provide feedback on a specific prototype. The prototype creators silently observe, taking notes, photographing, or videoing the experts' reactions and feedback. All questions asked by the experts are answered; however, the prototype is not defended or over-explained. The goal is to see what works, what doesn't, and what improvements are needed. Once the experts are finished and all feedback has been gathered, the Prototype Push is over.

Typical Scenario

Alexis needed expert feedback on her prototype. She identified three subject matter experts and invited them to test her prototype. She provided a simple lunch, and the experts ate as she introduced the prototype. Her guests then interacted with the prototype. Alexis answered their questions but, for the most part, observed. After about 15 minutes, an expert asked Alexis if she had any questions. She did, and they answered. In the end, Alexis felt the Prototype Push greatly improved the prototype. She thanked the participants for their contributions, then turned to her new information to review what she might need to change.

Question Quest

Try this to . . . evoke powerful questions.

Often, we can't find the answer because we don't understand the problem. Asking the right question makes all the difference, but asking questions is too often hard and scary. The Question Quest creates a way to ask powerful questions in a supportive environment.

Benefits

- Creates environment for hard questions to be asked

Resources Required

- Scribe to record questions and answers
- Whiteboard or large posters for writing
- Willing team committed to asking questions

How It Works

The group leader projects questions on a screen and reviews the problem or opportunity the group is addressing. Then, the leader divides participants into groups of four. While discussing the questions projected on the screen, the group is reminded to keep in mind the mother of all questions: what's *really* going on here? The questions on the screen could be:

- How do you know when the problem is present?
- What is keeping you or your team from solving the problem?
- Who can help solve this problem and isn't already involved?
- What ideas do you have that haven't already been shared or tried?
- What would be the first thing you noticed if the problem was solved?
- What actions are needed to get a solution moving?
- What needs to be done and by when?

After 45 minutes, the leader calls for the groups to share. A scribe is chosen to capture new ideas and thoughts as the groups share. The leader then thanks everyone and dismisses the group.

Typical Scenario

Keely and her team faced a challenge, so she gathered together a group that could help. First, she presented the problem to the group. She kept it at the 35,000-foot level so as to not limit the group's thinking. Next, she directed their attention to the questions projected on the screen. Keely asked participants to form groups of four and begin addressing the questions. At the end of the allotted time, Keely called for a volunteer scribe. Then, she asked the groups to share their most impactful idea or thought evoked by the questions. Once all the groups shared, she asked if anyone had anything else to add. Several team members asked additional questions. The scribe captured all questions and new thoughts. Keely was surprised at all the new perspectives. Several people said they liked wrestling with questions that pushed their thinking. One lady said she couldn't wait to run a Question Quest with her own group in the future.

Speed Empathy

Try this to . . . expedite learning about a problem from a wide variety of customers.

It's common for teams to face a challenge they don't really understand, yet they have to solve it anyway. They need to learn from those who are personally experiencing the problem. Speed Empathy is one way to accomplish this task.

Benefits

- Presents an effective way to gather needed information from customers or those experiencing the problem the team is trying to solve

Resources Required

- Five or more people who can share personal experiences about the challenge

- Bell
- Chairs
- Notepads
- Pencils
- Timer
- Timekeeper

How It Works

The goal of Speed Empathy is for Team A, the Empathizers (problem-solvers), to learn as much as possible from Team B, the Empathizees (people experiencing the problem).

Team A, the Empathizers, identifies at least five Empathizees and invites them to join Speed Empathy.

The room is arranged with two concentric circles of chairs. The inner circle of chairs faces the outer ring of chairs. Empathizers sit in the middle circle, and Empathizees sit in the outer circle. Empathizers face Empathizees.

The timekeeper explains the process.

- First, each Empathizer will be given five minutes to share personal experiences or stories they have had about the problem. Then, the Empathizers will ask the Empathizees a question, beginning with "Tell me about a time when . . . ," "What was your experience . . . ," etc.
- The Empathizers will take notes to capture emotions, pain points, new learnings, etc.
- Every five minutes, the timekeeper rings the bell, and the Empathizers stay put. The Empathizees all move one chair to the right.

Once all Empathizers have met with every Empathizee, time is called. Then, Empathizees are thanked for their time and dismissed.

The Empathizers are given 10 minutes to reflect individually, allowing new insights and learnings to bubble up. These thoughts and new insights are captured in the notebook. At the close of 10 minutes, the timekeeper calls the Empathizers back together. The group then spends 20 minutes sharing their new learnings and insights, captured on a whiteboard, blackboard, or a Google Workspace document. Once everyone has shared, the group identifies the uncovered needs. Finally, the knowledge and learnings gleaned from Speed Empathy are used to illuminate the real problem or specifics of an opportunity to create better solutions that are relevant and sustainable.

Typical Scenario

Sharon's nursing team needed to solve a COVID-related problem. So, Sharon invited nurses, unit clerks, and environmental services associates from the units experiencing the highest number of COVID patients to join her and the team for a Speed Empathy experience.

Sharon arranged the room in two circles and asked the invitees to sit in the inner circle. Sharon served as the timekeeper. Sharon's team listened to the stories and recorded the emotions to those in the inner circle. They were shocked by what they learned and how much they didn't know—all because they took the time to learn from those experiencing the problem. Sharon's team created a meaningful solution because of the new insights and empathy they gathered.

Threshold/Walk-Around Meetings

Try this to . . . access a top leader easily.

Threshold Meetings give quick access to a boss or leader and are perfect for those times when someone needs a quick yes or no. These are the perfect way to expedite a meeting when it might otherwise take days or weeks to get access.

Benefits

- Provides movement and access

Resources Required

- Leaders willing to try something new

How It Works

The boss must agree to the idea of a Threshold Meeting and the parameters. The boss's support staff is brought into the plan. Threshold Meetings only last a few seconds and usually require a one-word answer or a quick response. Threshold Meetings apply to projects that need ongoing input from a top leader or projects that will bog down without access to a leader.

A Threshold Meeting starts when someone from the project's team arrives at the boss's office. The support staff or admin alerts the boss. As soon as the boss can break away, they appear at their office door. The team member relays a message or makes their request. The boss answers, and the team member heads back to the project. However, if the boss feels more information is required, the admin will set up a longer meeting. The big win of Threshold Meetings is they keep things from bogging down when a simple answer will keep everything moving forward. Plus, these meetings free up a boss's schedule.

Another version of Threshold Meetings is Walk-Around Meetings. These meetings take advantage of a large campus where individuals must walk some distance to get from one location to another. So, for example, when an executive must walk to another meeting on another part of the campus, those who want a meeting can walk alongside them to discuss their needs, requests, or challenges.

Typical Scenario

Jack felt frustrated because he couldn't book a meeting with his senior vice president due to the VP's overfull schedule. So, Jack approached the VP's administrative assistant and asked if he could have just one minute of the VP's time. He told the administrative assistant that he would just stand at the threshold of the office door and not even sit down.

The assistant found a good time, and Jack showed up. He did just what he said he'd do: he stood at the doorway's threshold and took only one minute. The VP was so impressed with this idea that he suggested more employees do what Jack did. As a result, Jack was able to get the response he needed and move forward with his project.

SECTION SEVEN:

₰ Human-CENTERED Design with DESIGN THINKING TOOLS

Purpose:
Evoking human centered
thinking and solutions with
tools and activities.

Have you ever noticed how all of our problems are created by us humans? It's true! But the good news is that when we focus on putting people at the center of our solutions, we can come up with some really amazing ideas. It's kind of like blending science and art to find solutions that work for everyone.

One smart guy, Russell Ackoff, said that a system is not just the sum of its parts, but the result of how they all work together.[3]

And guess what? Anyone can be a human-centered design thinker! All you need is the right mindset, tools, and skills. That's where these cool human-centered engagements come in. They each represent a step in the design thinking process: empathy, define, ideation, prototype, and test. So, let's get creative and start solving some problems!

Empathy Expedition

Try this to . . . understand what the customer is experiencing.

When we can't find the answer, it's usually because we don't understand the problem we are trying to solve. The Empathy Expedition is the first step to understanding the problem. It's the process of going out and learning from those experiencing the problem. Learn from those people. Hear their stories. Observe them in their work setting. Listen to what they are saying. Answer the question: "What is really going on?"

Benefits

- Illuminates insights that help the designers understand the real problem

Resources Required

- People who are experiencing the problem

How It Works

Teams of two people go out to learn from customers. Each team identifies customers who are experiencing the problem and who they can learn from. One of the team members is the notetaker or photographer, and the other, designated the Talker, does the talking. The Talker asks the customer how they are experiencing the problem and invites them to share their story and experience. Wherever possible, the pair observes the customers in action, most importantly, to gather new insights and also to understand the customer experience, the pain points, what works, and what doesn't.

Typical Scenario

Isabella's team needed to understand why there were so many customer complaints. So, she asked her team to go out and experience what their customers experienced in order to build empathetic connections. Her team identified customers they could learn from and then met with them where they worked. They heard their stories, observed them in action, and wherever they could, experienced what the customers actually experienced. Team members worked in pairs and brought back surprising information. Isabella was proud of her team as they expressed over and over, "I never knew that!" and "Well, no wonder we couldn't fix the problem." The Empathy Expedition proved crucial to solving its long-time challenge.

Try this to . . . make sense out of the new learnings gathered during the Empathy Expedition.

Once the new insights and discoveries have been captured, it's time to make sense of all that you learned. The goal of the Empathy Unpack is to understand what the new insights mean, so the real needs can be identified.

Benefits

- Illuminates the real need(s) of the customer and the heart of the problem

Resources

- Time for unpacking the empathy gained
- Whiteboard or large poster for writing

How It works

Use the following categories to make sense of new information and discoveries the team gathered:

- *Step 1*: Answer the following questions:
  - Scenes: What did you observe?
  - Stories: Who shared? What did they share?
  - Quotes: What soundbites did you hear that captured the expressed emotions?
  - Patterns: What was consistent?
- *Step 2*: The team works to identify obvious and hidden needs in the answers to the above questions.
- *Step 3*: The needs are listed.
- *Step 4*: The team votes on the needs they feel they can best address.
- *Step 5*: One or several needs are chosen.
- *Step 6*: The team now decides the next steps.

Feet Voting

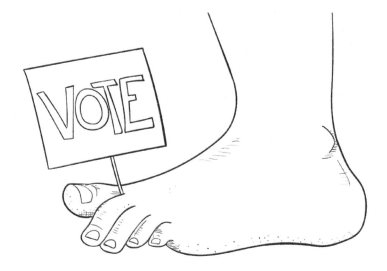

Try this to . . . provide a way for people to let their preferences be known.

When people need to choose between several options, Feet Voting is a great choice. It is an engaging yet efficient way to help people choose what they really want.

Benefits

- Provides a way for participants to disagree, express conflicting ideas, or have different interests while still collaborating

Resources Required

- Big Post-its or whiteboards
- Large group of people to vote
- Various challenges

How It Works

For those times when team members must individually decide between several viable ideas, Feet Voting can be helpful. First, the ideas are each written on a different poster or paper and placed around the room. Then, participants are asked to choose which idea they want by walking over and standing beside the idea.

This tool can also be used in a virtual meeting through polling or paired with virtual breakouts where topics can be discussed by paying attention to differences.

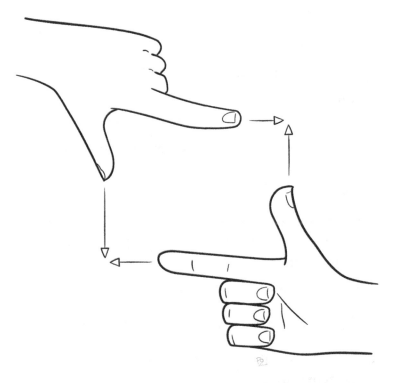

Try this to . . . create a design challenge to frame a challenge or problem.

Successful projects have well-crafted challenge statements that frame the problem in a balanced way and keep the scope from being too broad or narrow. Design thinkers refer to such statements as "How Might We (HMW) statements."

Benefits

- Creates a platform for considering many solutions and scenarios while still providing a balanced scope

How It Works

Begin by answering questions in two distinct parts:

Part 1

1. What problems exist within the system?
2. What undesirable outcomes are these problems causing?

Part 2

1. What is the perfect future state of the system?
2. What outcomes would be beneficial to all within the system?
3. Who is at the heart of this system?

Once you have your answers, fill out this template:

How might we shift from a system that _____ to a system that _____?

The idea is to tweak and work with the statement so it creates an overarching guide for your project. Keep in mind that all good challenge statements are revisited, refocused, and refined as the project proceeds.

Learn, Unlearn, Relearn

Try this to . . . help a team understand what to do when disruption occurs.

Alvin Toffler rightly said, "The illiterate of the 21st century will not be those who cannot read or write, but those who cannot learn, unlearn, and relearn."[4] This engagement helps us do just that.

Benefits

- Raises awareness of the nature of disruption

Resources Required

- Large posters
- Stickers for voting
- Paper for individual writing
- Sharpies

How It Works

A facilitator or guide asks, "In today's post-pandemic world what do we need to *learn, unlearn,* and *relearn*?" Once the question is asked, the facilitator or guide leads the group through the following steps:

1. The facilitator invites everyone to take a few minutes and identify at least two things the team needs to learn, unlearn, and relearn (two minutes).

2. Next, everyone pairs off and shares their ideas (eight minutes).

3. Then, the facilitator asks each pair to join another pair to form a group of four. Everyone shares their thoughts (15 minutes).

4. Finally, the facilitator asks each group to choose a spokesperson and a scribe.

5. Then, each group prepares to share their ideas while the scribe writes and captures the thoughts on a large poster.

6. Now it's time for the group share-out. A spokesperson for each group shares the group's ideas until all groups have shared.

7. Time is then given for everyone to individually review the posters and vote for the ideas they believe have the most potential. Each person gets three votes. Use stickers or Sharpies for marking ideas.

8. Once the voting is complete and the votes are tallied, the guide shares the results with the group.

9. Next steps are identified for the chosen idea.

10. Finally, a follow-up meeting is scheduled to discuss progress.

Powerful Personas

PHYSICIAN   BREAST CARE COORDINATOR   RAD   SCHEDULER   TECH

Try this to . . . better understand customer demographics.

Personas are fictional characters created to help a team understand the groups of people they serve. Every innovator knows you cannot create relevant solutions until you first understand the people for whom you are problem-solving and creating a solution. This isn't always easy! Powerful Personas is a proven and viable way to capture customer or end-user needs.

Benefits

- Clarifies population segments, highlights patterns, and identifies unspoken needs

Resources Required

- Felt pens or drawing instruments
- Large paper or whiteboard to create personas
- Time to learn from those who experience the problem

How It Works

In this activity, participants will identify specific personas present within a group. A persona is the aspect of someone's character that is presented to or perceived by others. Each persona represents a common characteristic, talent, or skill people embody. Follow these steps to identify powerful personas:

- *Step 1*: Working individually or in a group, participants begin by creating a preliminary list of people in the population they are studying. For example, for a project helping a school, personas could be created from these population segments: administrators, teachers, coaches, parents, students, support staff, volunteers, etc. More segments can be added as more information is gathered.

- *Step 2*: The team takes these population segments and identifies specific characteristics within each. Examples could include new teachers and veteran teachers; neurotypical students and neurodivergent students; bus drivers and cafeteria staff; etc.

- *Step 3*: Create a graphic to represent each population segment.

- *Step 4*: The team reviews and studies each persona. As they review, create questions to debunk false assumptions about population segments and help expose unidentified needs.

- *Step 6*: The team lists both spoken and unspoken needs.
- *Step 7*: The needs are made visible for the team and stakeholders to see.

Typical Scenario

Thomas believed Powerful Personas would provide his team the insights they needed to create the best possible solution. Since the challenge and target population were large, Thomas and his team went on-site to connect with customers. They observed, heard stories, and asked questions.

After they felt they had a good idea of their customers, they returned to unpack their findings. From their learnings, they created six personas: insured older patients, uninsured older patients, insured single patients, uninsured single patients, insured young parents, and uninsured young parents. Each persona had a story behind it, packed with specifics that represented the similarities within each group. These personas were hand-drawn and stood about six feet tall. Next, team members brought the personas to the larger innovation project team.

The personas guided and inspired discussions, helped define the real problem, and aided in idea generation and creating prototypes. As a result, the team believed it had made more relevant final solutions and more effectively addressed critical elements of its challenge because it used these personas.

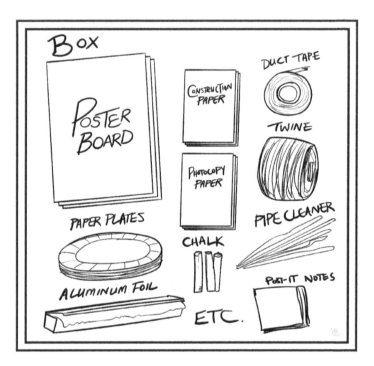

Try this to ... keep materials on hand for easy prototyping.

Some say the biggest problem with prototyping is we don't do it often enough. However, I believe people would if they had the materials on hand to do so. The Prototype Kit can provide any team with essential supplies for almost any low-resolution prototype. Many ideas are hard to understand or can't always be adequately visualized. This can lead either to shutting down the idea and its potential or to half-baked solutions that don't address the problem. The Prototype Kit and Rapid Prototyping can help clarify these ideas.

Benefits

- Makes prototyping possible and easy to do

Resources Required

- Aluminum foil
- Chalk
- Construction paper
- Duct tape in multiple colors and sizes
- Paper plates
- Poster board
- Photocopy paper
- Pipe cleaners
- Simple box to carry or store materials
- Twine
- Anything else needed for the specific prototype

How It Works

The key to good prototyping is summarized in three words: rough, rapid, and right.

- Rapid: Always create low resolutions prototypes quickly.
- Rough: Keep the prototypes rough. Remember, they are low resolution.
- Right: The prototype must be right for the idea you are trying to test.

A prototype can be a physical artifact you can hold, storyboard, skit, or roleplay.

Try this to . . . see a problem in a new light or from a different perspective.

A team may think they have defined a problem, but if given an opportunity, they could see the problem might be more multifaceted than they originally believed. Teams typically don't get that opportunity.

Benefits

- Gives new perspective on a problem, challenge, or opportunity

Resources Required

- Problem or opportunity

How It Works

Once a team has stated a problem and has not yet thrown out any solutions, the group takes a few minutes to ask the following questions:

- What's missing?
- Is the situation we are focusing on really the most pressing issue?
- What's currently working?
- How does what's working relate to the problem or opportunity?
- What am I presently doing that contributes to this problem or opportunity?
- What do those who are experiencing the issue say about it?

Typical Scenario

Vasthi faced a problem. She called her team together, explained the issue, and before anyone tried to solve it or suggested any solutions, she pulled out the RRR questions and asked each one.

The team spent at least two minutes on each question and discovered that what they had assumed was the core problem was only part of the issue. After going through the questions, they could fully see the situation and define it better.

Rights for Creators

Try this to . . . get a team unstuck and give agency to every team member.

Often, the best ideas come from front-line staff or those doing the actual work. Those team members need permission and agency to share their ideas. Rights for Creators gives everyone on the team a voice, especially in times when new ideas are most needed.

Benefits

- Encourages teams to learn from failures

Resources Required

- Courageous team members
- Willing team

101 Activities to Ignite Collaboration, Boost Creativity, and Fuel Innovation

How It Works

When a team is stuck or a looming deadline has everyone stymied, any team member who has a new idea calls out, "Rights for Creators!" This phrase means a team member has a new idea or perspective they want to share. The person usually calls out when the team isn't ideating.

When the call is heard, everyone stops. The person who makes the call shares their new idea or solution. Even if the individual is not a team leader, the team takes the time to listen and see if the new idea has merit. If it does, they act upon it. If it doesn't, the group returns to their work. The idea behind Rights for Creators is to interrupt what is happening, so a new idea can be expressed.

Typical Scenario

While Samantha did not serve as the lead on a project, she believed her team was heading in the wrong direction. "I call 'Rights for Creators,'" she said, and the group invited her to share her idea. This felt like a big stretch for Samantha because she didn't often take the lead, but because the whole team had agreed to Rights for Creators, everyone cooperated. The group stopped, listened to Samantha, and decided to try the idea. Team energy rose, participants embraced the new views, and the project began moving forward in a more positive direction.

Try this to . . . bring several teams or departments together into a collective understanding.

As they say, "teamwork makes the dream work." That's true . . . until silos destroy it all. How many times have you seen teams crippled, morale destroyed, and people quit all because of silos? Silos are a problem. However, with Silo Storming, that can change today!

Benefits

- Creates understanding and collaboration among different departments or teams

Resources Required

- Guide to facilitate Silo Storming
- Neutral place to meet

How it Works

- *Step 1:* A neutral venue or location in the organization is chosen for Silo Storming. Several departments meet together and sit according to their departments.

- *Step 2:* For 10 minutes, each department lists its strengths, weaknesses, and a current problem it is experiencing.

- *Step 3:* Each department is invited to share its responses with the whole group. A brief Q&A follows. The guide captures the team's request for help.

- *Step 4:* Once every department has shared, all requests for help are reviewed. Any team that wants to help another team solve its problem speaks up. Arrangements are made for the next steps.

- *Step 5:* Next, the whole group identifies new learnings.

- *Step 6:* The Silo Storming session ends with a short reflection focused on the following questions:
  - What new learnings were gained?
  - What viable next steps are needed?

- *Step 7:* The guide thanks everyone for coming and bids everyone farewell.

Story Snippet

Try this to . . . tell your story graphically.

Story Snippets are short stories that share how ordinary people solved specific problems or embraced an emerging opportunity.

Discovery

Sense-Makings

The Big Shift

Creation

Benefits
- Presents a quick way for a team or company to capture accomplishments or news

Resources Required
- Large paper, poster, or whiteboard
- One-page summary of a completed innovation project
- Printed photos or graphics
- Writing utensils

How It Works

After completing a project, the team creates a one-page summary, adding graphics or photos to highlight vital elements and brighten the page. Each Story Snippet includes the challenge (the problem or opportunity), new discoveries (what the team learned), the solution (any new ideas), and the outcome (results or feedback).

The format follows these statements:

- We thought the problem was _____.
- We were surprised to lean _____.
- So, we created _____.
- When we showed people, they said, "_____ _____."
- This was our outcome and solution: _____ _____.
- Our world was changed by _____.

Try this to . . . test an idea or solution and get feedback.

When a team needs to know if they are on the right track, Testing 101 can provide valuable insights and learnings.

TESTING 101

Build your Prototype

Create a Plan

Identify testers

Rehearse

Record Findings

Share-out

Benefits

- Provides feedback and insights into the validity of an idea and ideas for next iterations

Resources Required

- Notebook and writing instrument
- Phone or camera
- Time for testing

How It Works

Use the template to help you design a testing plan for an idea or solutions you have created.

- *Step 1*: Build a very rough prototype that represents your idea or solution and that your end-user or customer can interact with.
- *Step 2*: Create your testing plan by answering:
  - What will the testing include?
  - When will the test take place?
  - Where will the test happen?
  - Which question will evoke relevant feedback?
  - How will you arrange the testing experience?
- *Step 3*: Identify those invited to be in the testing experience. Who are they?
- *Step 4*: Practice your testing experience. Make sure your instructions are clear and will provide the result you want.
- *Step 5*: Run your prototype, and record the feedback gathered.
- *Step 6*: Share the results of your Testing 101 experience.

WHO Will Do WHAT By WHEN (W³)?

(who)
will do (what?)
by (when?)

Try this to . . . assign next steps.

We've all heard the adage: "No job is done until the paperwork is done." The same goes for projects. They're not done until everyone on the team knows WHO Will Do WHAT By WHEN (W³). The team collectively completes the W³, so everyone knows their next steps. It's a straightforward way to tie up a meeting or project, so everyone knows what is happening. Plus, people feel a sense of satisfaction, knowing that follow-up will happen.

Benefits

- Clarifies next steps and provides closure for a project, meeting, or discussion

Resources Required

- W³ form

How It Works

As the final step of a project, planning session, or anything that requires follow-up, the leader, guide, or facilitator brings out the WHO Will Do WHAT By WHEN tool (W^3).

- W^3 = **WHO** Will Do **WHAT** By **WHEN**

Typical Scenario

Doug's team came to the final stages of a project. The next step was to implement some of the solutions. First, the team used the W^3 form to determine what tasks still needed to be accomplished. Next, the team assigned specific individuals to complete the required tasks and developed a timeline that stated when each task needed to be done.

Section Eight:
Reflection Tools

Purpose:

Developing competency in reflective practices to drive deeper learning.

You know what they say: "No reflection, no learning!" Why not make reflecting a part of our everyday routine? I've heard from clients and students that they absolutely loved learning about reflection. Not only did it make their workshops and courses more meaningful, but it was also a blast and super relaxing.

Leaders out there, listen up! When you make reflection a part of your personal and professional routine, you give a gift that can't be measured. It's great for you and your team.

Now, don't worry if you're not sure how to get started with reflecting. It's as simple as asking yourself some questions like: what new thing did I learn today? What surprised me about this experience? What can I take away from this? And how can I use this new insight to improve my work?

Let's all work together to make reflection less intimidating and more accessible to everyone!

101 Activities to Ignite Collaboration, Boost Creativity, and Fuel Innovation

No Shame, No Blame Game

Try this to . . . give a team time to reflect and reframe.

Teams fail. People fail. And when failure happens, shame and blame can start flying every which way. However, failure is the flip side of success, so if we want to be successful, failure is inevitable. That's why reflection is so important. Building competency in reflective practice is a pillar of a happy, meaningful life. The No Shame, No Blame Game is here to help.

Benefits

- Creates space for reflection and reframing when someone or a team failed or things didn't go as planned

How It Works

When a team experiences failure or when something doesn't go as planned, a member of the team, the host, calls for a three-minute No Shame, No Blame Game. First, the host asks for someone to share what went wrong or what happened. A quick Q&A follows the explanation. The team then explores how they might do things differently next time so as not to repeat the failure or mistake.

Typical Scenario

Morgan facilitated an on-site innovation project and forgot to bring prototype materials. The team was on a fast track to report its project solutions to top leaders, but unfortunately, without the necessary materials, the team couldn't create a viable prototype. Some group members believed the report couldn't go forward without it.

Morgan saw it as a big failure: "Wow, we really blew it." However, the team already agreed to a No Shame, No Blame Game, and it quickly pivoted to thinking about what it might do to move forward. Team members also asked one another, "What might we do differently next time?" One great lesson came from this mistake: from then on, prototype materials were put in a box near every innovation group before the group started its work.

Ponder Points

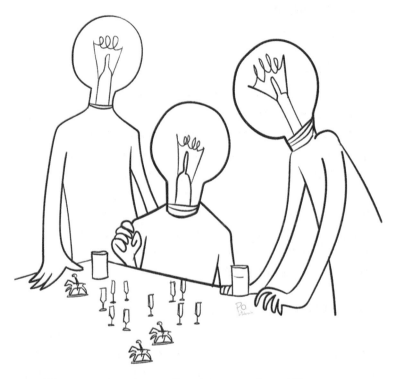

Try this to . . . develop reflective practice skills.

A chief nursing officer at a large healthcare system once told me, "Our biggest problem today is that we have no time to think." This is a scary statement in light of everything happening in healthcare, politics, and the economy! More than ever, we need designated time for introspection, which is why I created Ponder Points.

Benefits

- Builds reflection skills

Resources Required

- Quiet place

How It Works

Set aside three minutes a day to ponder. You can shut your office door, stroll, or hide under your desk. The key is to schedule the time, set a reminder alarm, and stick to precisely three minutes. Excuse yourself when your Ponder Point time arrives; you don't have to explain. (Maybe your colleagues think you're using the restroom.) Step away, shut your eyes, and breathe. This exercise has no required topic or next steps. If three minutes is too much, start with one minute. There is no one right way. Just give yourself time to think!

Typical Scenario

Cathy felt overwhelmed with her workload; however, she embraced Ponder Points. Each morning at 10:45 a.m., she stepped away from her regular duties and out to a small side garden outside her office. She set the timer on her phone for three minutes, closed her eyes, and thought. When her phone alarm went off, she returned to everyday tasks. After a few days, she found herself looking forward to these times and told a friend, "On the days when I ponder, I think clearer, feel calmer, and actually get more done."

Stinky Fish and Catch of the Day

Try this to . . . provide a way to manage fears around a project or event.

Innovation can strike fear in even the stoutest of hearts. When fear ensues, people shut down, act up, freak out, or turn in. They hold fast to their business-as-usual mindsets. Stinky Fish might be just what they need.

This is a fun, funky pre-project or post-project assessment that gets people to talk about their fears. The goal is to help each person reduce their fears or even replace them with new and more effective ways of thinking. The Stinky Fish activity pairs well with innovation projects that tend to be political or that tread on other "sacred" or otherwise controversial grounds.

Benefits

- Addresses and normalizes fears by putting fears in context

Resources Required

- Large Post-its
- Sharpies

How It Works

Launch the Stinky Fish activity at the beginning of the project. Give each participant a large Post-it Note. Have each team member draw their own version of a Stinky Fish and list their fears about the project below the drawing. Then, invite members to share their fears with the larger group.

As the project proceeds, ask participants to revisit their fish drawing and adjust their fears according to their new learnings or insights. At the end of the project, invite team members to revisit their Stinky Fish and see if their fears have subsided. If so, the Stinky Fish transforms into a Catch of the Day. Each participant shares the status of their Stinky Fish. Did it morph into a Catch of the Day, or did it remain a Stinky Fish? Either way, participants share new insights and learnings.

Typical Scenario

Nathalie and her team feared their project would ostracize their coworkers. So, the facilitator invited Nathalie and her team to grab large Post-it Notes and stick them on the wall around the room. Then, each group member was instructed to use a Sharpie to draw a Stinky Fish.

When everyone finished, the facilitator asked participants to write their fears about the project below their fish. Most quickly began writing. "I need a bigger paper to capture all my fears," someone yelled.

The team laughed but kept writing—all but a person named Olive. She had sketched a decent-looking fish but hesitated to write down any fears. "I'm uncomfortable putting my fears out in the open," she said. "If my boss comes by, I might get fired."

Laughing and joking ensued as team members voiced their fears. "Oh, I can relate to that fear," said one.

"Wow, I've never looked at the problem from a fearful mindset," declared another. Not everyone was joking, however. Some wrote quietly while Olive continued to stand there, staring at her fish.

After a bit, the facilitator called everyone back together: "Anyone want to share their fears?"

"I was afraid we couldn't be honest," admitted one.

"That the leaders wouldn't listen," said another.

"That we wouldn't be able to implement our ideas or solutions," declared a third.

People nodded in agreement as various members admitted their fears—everyone, that is, except Olive. "I'm afraid I'm going to be fired once this project is completed," she finally said. When team members asked Olive to elaborate, she hesitated but then shared her fear.

After each project phase, team members were encouraged to revisit their fish and see whether their new insights helped abate those fears. "Are your assumptions still accurate?" the facilitator asked. "Did you learn anything that ended your fear?"

At the close of the project, team members reflected on how their perspectives had changed. Members described their new findings and explained how their Stinky Fish had become the Catch of the Day. To everyone's surprise, Olive spoke first.

"I thought this was a strange activity when the project began," Olive admitted, "but after considering what I learned in this project and using those insights against my fears, I realized I had misjudged my boss. I believed the lies I was telling myself." This exercise helped Olive *reel* in her fears with a clearer mindset.

In the end, the team felt that, by articulating their fears, it was possible to address them as a group and work through them in a way that benefited everyone.

Time to Choose Our Spokesperson

Try this to . . . choose a spokesperson for small groups in a fun way.

When a spokesman for a small or large group is needed, this is a quick, fun way to choose a person in a matter of moments.

Benefits

- Provides potential for quieter members to be showcased

Resources Required

- Guide

How It Works

Time to Choose Our Spokesperson couldn't be simpler. First, announce that each of the small groups you are working with will each need a spokesperson. Then, immediately ask everyone to close their eyes and point to someone in the group. When you ask everyone to open their eyes, the person with the most people pointing to them is the spokesperson.

Try this to . . . provide an interactive group reflection.

Without reflection, there is no learning. Educators everywhere know that if we want to create relevant solutions, we need to reflect. Unfortunately, life's business often crowds out time for introspection. The result? Unrealized potential. The Totally Awesome Sense-Making engagement helps infuse reflection into daily teamwork and projects.

Benefits

- Activates the whole group in reflection

Resources Required

- People willing to reflect
- Time

How It Works

At the end of a project or an event, a guide invites team members to think quietly and consider what lessons can be drawn from what was just experienced for 30 seconds. Then, the guide invites participants to pair up with someone else in the group. Pairs have two minutes to share their thoughts. When the timer goes off, the guide invites each pair to connect with another pair and exchange their thoughts for five minutes. The guide then calls for a group share-out and looks for three or four people to share.

What're Ya Thinkin'?

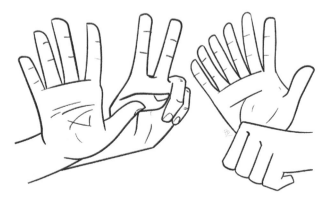

Try this to . . . to check a team's engagement.

When you want to know just how engaged a team is, the What're Ya Thinkin'? tool might be what you need.

Benefits

- Checks everyone's level of engagement and allows for adjustments

Resources Required

- Fingers

How It Works

This tool is used when you want to check a team's engagement levels and hear what team members are thinking and feeling. First, when it looks like members are fading or checked out, the group leader calls for a "finger check" and asks members to hold up the number of fingers that shows how engaged they are, 10 being the highest and one being the lowest.

The leader counts backward from three (three, two, one), and everyone holds up their fingers. Then, the leader asked those holding up only a few fingers, "What do you need to get to a 10?"

SECTION NINE:

Knock-their-SOCKS-OFF!! Presentations

Purpose:
Creating stellar presentations that keep people talking long after the workshop ends.

Oh boy, have you heard what American poet Richard Armour said? "I love a finished speaker. I really, truly do. And I don't mean one who's polished, I just mean one who's *through*."[5] And who can blame him? We all love it when a presentation doesn't drag on or bore us with endless PowerPoint slides. Everyone wants a presentation to end on a high note.

If you want to wow your audience and keep them hanging on to your every word, it's all about knowing what they want and delivering it with pizzazz. And don't worry; you don't need to be some fancy, polished speaker to do it. Just stick to the simple tips in this section, and you'll have everyone begging for an encore! Let's flex those presentation muscles and get ready to soar!

Call It Out

Try this to . . . name the elephant in the room.

Have you ever run a workshop or given a talk when half of the audience got "volun-told" to be there? Yeah, it's the pits! Before you pack up and go home, remember it's not personal. The best way forward is to simply acknowledge it. Let the people know you sympathize with them and will do your best to make the presentation fun. People will like you, if not love you, for it.

Benefits

- Addresses the elephant in the room

Resources Required

- Courageous speaker
- Bored audience

How It works

This is an easy one. If you get the sense that the audience is there because of a boss's mandate, don't pretend you don't know or notice. Instead, ask, "How many of you have been required to be here today?" Or, "How many of you would rather be somewhere else?"

You could even start with, "Who already knows all the information I'm about to present? Let's see a show of hands." Then, when people raise their hands, say, "Thank you for your honesty. First off, I feel your pain. I'll do my best to make this worthwhile because I've been in your shoes! Let's do a quick tally for those of you who already know a lot about this topic."

Then, ask people, "What do you already know about the subject?" Have a scribe capture what is shared. Then, ask the rest of the audience if they already know this too. If so, call for questions that people are interested in. This might sound unproductive, but believe me, it can make all the difference.

Knock Their Socks Off

Try this to . . . create a workshop or presentation that resonates.

You've been asked to give a presentation. "Yikes!" you exclaim. "What will I say?" Or maybe you don't know how to put a compelling presentation tougher, don't have time to prepare, or don't know what to say. Whatever the case, try Knock Their Socks Off for a dynamic and engaging presentation.

Benefits

- Demystifies presentation creation

Resources Required

- Audience
- Presentation to prepare

How It Works

Presentations ripe with boring elements put people to sleep, cause daydreams, or the most blatant of all, make people pull out their phones. However, simple guidelines can pull any presentation out of the doldrums.

- Choose a very specific, compelling topic the audience relates to.
  - Take time to understand who you are speaking to. Who is your audience? What are their interests, pain points, needs, etc.? Identify what really matters to them, and speak on that point. For example, I was speaking to a group of new

leaders who wanted to learn how to become more collaborative, so I chose the topic "Two Words Can Change Your Life: Yes And . . ."

- Have one main point; develop only *one* specific idea or topic.
  - Keep your talk simple and short. Give your lecture, and share the valuable lessons that are core to the workshop. Forget sharing everything you know. Instead, highlight a particular topic. For example, instead of labeling your presentation "How to Be an Innovative Thinker," title it "Two Words Can Change Your Life: Yes And . . ."
- Create a soundbite.
  - Come up with a simple, easy-to-remember soundbite that supports your topic and illuminates what it means. Make it bold and punchy. For example:
    - Every idea deserves three seconds of life.
    - There's no such thing as a bad idea.
    - Say "yes, and . . ."
- Tell a story.
  - Tell a personal story, or show a short video that supports your main points. Make it personal and real. People love real stories that support the main point. In my presentation, I told the story of how my fourth-grade teacher taught me "yes, and . . ."

- Run a quick engagement that gets audiences on their feet.
  - Check out the other engagements in this book. Find the one that best suits your topic. Get your audience moving and involved. For example, I used the Paired Story engagement.
- Lead a super short reflection.
  - Invite your audience to reflect on how the engagement relates to your topic. Drive the main point of your presentation deeper by having the audience identify new learnings and insights. Check out engagements 96-101.
- Challenge your audience.
  - Send your audience home with a compelling challenge. Ask your audience how they might apply what they've learned both professionally and personally. Give them a time frame. For example: "Before the sun sets tonight, say 'yes, and . . .' in three different situations."

A Three-Step Variation

This is a much simpler version that includes three simple elements: your story, one point, and a call to action.

The presentation begins with your story, a well-crafted narrative that supports or illuminates your main point. After the story, head straight into your one main point. With that point made, challenge your audience to do some specific thing.

Workshops That Work (WTW)

Try this to . . . create a memorable workshop.

The challenge with many workshops is that participants aren't easily able to apply the information in a meaningful way either professionally or personally. Once the workshop is over, most of the learning dissipates with it. If workshop attendees cannot apply the information in a sustainable way, why attend?

That's why I developed the Workshops That Work (WTW) formula—to create workshops that make information relevant, manageable, and applicable. Otherwise, workshops are just an excuse for people to cram into a room, endure a PowerPoint, drink coffee, and write in some journal they picked up at the registration desk. Let's dive into WTW.

Benefits

- Demystifies workshop creation

Resources Required

- Scribe willing to note everyone's mantras
- Simple assessment and post-assessment activities
- Participants willing to engage in an interactive workshop
- Prototyping materials, such as paper, poster board, and craft supplies

How It Works

- Begin a workshop with a simple assessment that is followed up with a post-assessment. This heightens everyone's experience and drives learning. Remember to have participants return to their pre-assessment to note changes or new learnings.

- Keep lectures short. Get the audience involved in interactive learning engagements, personal stories, and fun graphics as soon and as much as possible. I like to keep a 25-75 ratio. I talk 25 percent of the time and have the audience actively involved 75 percent of the time.

- Offer reflection opportunities throughout the workshop. Remember, there is no real learning without reflection. Include a reflection in every engagement. Ask, "What lessons can we draw from this experience that we can apply professionally and or personally?"

- Let participants share their thoughts after reflections. Have someone capture these reflections that can be posted on a wall or somewhere everyone can see.

- Allow time for prototyping. Have simple materials on hand, so participants can create a visual representation (prototype) of their new learnings.

- Allow participants to share their prototypes. Ask, "What do the prototypes mean? How will they be applied professionally or personally?"

- Give the audience 30 seconds to create mantras or soundbites around their prototype.

- The group ends with a collective check-out, simply saying, "One, two, three . . . I'm _____, and I'm checking out."

- Once the workshop is over, hang around because there will inevitably be people who want to share, ask questions, or get advice.

101 Activities to Ignite Collaboration, Boost Creativity, and Fuel Innovation

Four-Minute Report-Out

Try this to . . . deliver important information in a super short, comprehensive format.

Four-Minute Report-Out is a fast, efficient way to present project outcomes in an engaging manner.

Benefits

- Gets new information to top leaders in a fast and compelling way

Resources Required

- Feedback grid for report-out panel
- Report-out panel comprised of four to five decision-makers
- Report-out presentation form
- Prototype

How It Works

Four-Minute Report-Out Template:

- Team members introduce themselves in one sentence
- Project name
- Inciting incident
- New insights
- Ideas for solutions
- Prototype type
- Plan for testing or feedback from testing

The team members introduce themselves and the project name. They take turns sharing the information on the Four-Minute Report-Out Template. At the close, the report-out panel is invited to ask questions and provide feedback on what its members liked, what they would like to see changed, and new ideas they might have.

101 Activities to Ignite Collaboration, Boost Creativity, and Fuel Innovation

Conclusion

As you probably know by now, I totally believe in these engagement activities! One time, I was sitting in the audience waiting for a program to start, and this awesome lady tapped me on the shoulder and said, "Hey Karen, I was in one of your workshops, and it changed the way I see work and life!" How cool is that?

I love hearing feedback like that from my past students and workshop participants because I know my exercises are working. Whenever I work with organizations, I always urge everyone to try out these activities with their teams. If they work, awesome! If not, that's okay too. But you have to give it a shot, right?

I'm a big fan of experiential learning, and this book is all about that! The activities in it are fun, a bit crazy, and totally over the top. That's what helps people break down their walls and build trust with their colleagues. **If you want to execute creative projects successfully, you have to be open-minded and reflective and ask questions without getting defensive.** That can be tough, but these activities are designed to help you step out of your comfort zone and fully engage in the creative process with your team.

My hope is that, after reading this book, leaders and workers will realize that **there's always a solution to any challenge.** Traditional problem-solving methods are outdated. Instead, help your teams open their minds, hearts, and wills to achieve real, sustainable change. And when we stop taking ourselves too seriously, we can all become more curious, compassionate, and courageous leaders. Yay for creativity and collaboration! Let's keep inspiring each other!

Acknowledgments

We just wanted to give a huge shoutout to all the amazing folks who have joined us on this wild ride. From the doctors and nurses to the teachers and business peeps to everyone in between who tried out our engagements—you guys are the best! I know some of our activities were pretty out there, but you all jumped in (even if it was reluctantly) and had a blast (or at least a chuckle) along the way. And let's not forget about all the invaluable feedback you gave us—we couldn't have done it without you!

And to all the other creatives who create awesome stuff and concoct amazing activities daily: we all know some of our activities might be similar to others. Many times, we designed an engagement, thinking we had created something original, only to wait a week or two and learn some other groups had created something very similar. It's true what they say: "There's nothing new under the sun." But it's all about how you bring it to life, am I right?

And of course, we can't forget where it all began and with who. So, we give a heartfelt thank you to all of the fantabulous innovation lab team members who also made this book possible: Thomas Aldinger, Katherine Beckner, Molly Braga, Isabela Caicedo, Michelle Cocita, Vashti Daly, Keely DeGroot, Morgan Hamby, Lauren Heinrich, Christoph Hermann, Jordan Jones, Kyle Koszuta, Enoc Lopez, Brian Mayrsohn, Alexis Meeks, Matias Meiralles Van Vilet, Lisa B. Miller, Sunita Patolia, Richard Paul, Juliana Sarah, Amanda Saunders, Jordan Soliday,

Christian Spinella, Trevor Swanson, Andy Tilstra, David Tilstra, and Cecil Wiese.

I, Karen, also want to recognize these wonderful creatives:

- To my parents who had more than 101 ways to successfully propel their five children to adulthood;
- To my siblings, Debbie, Cheryl, Elise, and David, who are tributes to creativity;
- To my boys, Matthew, David, and Andy, who live out three distinct aspects of creativity;
- To my daughter-in-laws, Lourdes and Nicole, who help me see new perspectives;
- To my precious grandchildren, Adriana and Liam, who remind me to wonder;
- To my uncle Don and uncle Ron who taught me, at a very young age, the art of swimming in a canal;
- To Dan, my dear husband, who has to be the most creative person in the whole wide world.

Patrick acknowledges these wonderful people:

- To my wife, Meredith, and my children, Michael and Felicity, whose love and support inspires me every day;
- To my mom, dad, and brother who I thank for a childhood filled with nature and creativity.

And thank you to the formidable Steve Haliday, Jamie Fleming, Nicholas Aguirre, Zoe Rose, and Janelle Kay who pushed us over the finish line!

Keep inspiring creativity wherever you are!

Karen and Patrick

Notes

1. David Aycan, "Innovation Thrives Under These 5 Evidence-Backed Conditions," September 3, 2019, www.ideo.com/journal/innovation-thrives-under-these-5-evidence-backed-conditions.

2. Marshall Goldsmith, "Try Feedforward Instead of Feedback," accessed March 31, 2023, marshallgoldsmith.com/articles/try-feedforward-instead-feedback/.

3. Russel L. Ackoff, "Systems thinking and thinking systems," *Systems Dynamic Review* 10, nos. 2-3 (1994): 175-188, www.iwp.edu/wp-content/uploads/2019/05/20140905_AckoffSystemsThinkingandThinkingSystems.pdf.

4. Susan Ratcliffe, ed. *Oxford Essential Quotations*, 4th ed. (Oxford: University of Oxford Press, 2016).

5. Malcolm Kushner, *Presentations for Dummies* (Hoboken, NJ: Wiley, 2004).

About the Author

Dr. Karen Tilstra is a renowned innovator, entrepreneur, and thought leader in the field of design thinking, creativity, and innovation. As the founder and president of the Creativity Effect, Karen has spent the past decade creating innovation labs and developing design thinking teams for healthcare systems, government agencies, universities, and Fortune 500 companies.

Karen has a track record of success in innovation, having facilitated hundreds of design thinking projects for more than 37 national and international companies, winning three innovation awards in the process. She has presented at TEDx events twice and has spoken nationally and internationally.

Karen's passion for innovation and creativity is evident in all that she does, including co-designing the nation's first undergraduate degree in innovation and social entrepreneurship at Rollins College in Winter Park, Florida. She has served as a faculty member, Executive Fellow for Innovation, and on innovation advisory boards in the USA, Europe, and Asia.

Karen is the author of *The Deathline: Stopping the #1 All-Time Killer of Human Potential*.

She currently resides in Florida with her husband, and they are both rejoicing that their three sons have successfully launched into the big, wide world.

About the Artist

Patrick O'Connor is a Canadian/American designer, illustrator, dad, and all-around nice guy. He learned to cross-country ski before he could walk, taught Floridian tourists how to do moose calls, and worked in an innovation lab. A self-taught extrovert, he thanks tabletop roleplaying for helping him make friends and is somehow married with two children.

Made in the USA
Monee, IL
09 November 2023

46102051R00155